"As a business coach, I tell potential clie
have 'done it before' and several times a
qualify The Real Jason Duncan as an e
significant management systems inside you
the core aspects of your greatest talents. In Jason's book: you
the author lays out a clear process to first understand the required challenges ahead, then systematically put processes and people in place that allow you to have a certain kind of lifestyle, one we all strive for, as an entrepreneur.

Ultimately, this book guides you through how to live the exit lifestyle while maintaining ownership of your business. achieving the best of both worlds: a profitable and growing business as well as the ability to live your ideal lifestyle – without the need to put in insane hours and stay in the weeds every day.

The end result is a happier life, more family time and a more satisfying outcome than the traditional entrepreneurial journey. I highly recommend Jason's guidance and this book is a great place to start your journey to live the exit lifestyle."

- ***Mitch Russo***, *Founder, Coach, Author*

"The Real Jason Duncan is one of those people you meet and say 'I wish I met him before I screwed things up'. Exit without Exiting is not a luxury, it's a necessity for the entrepreneur that wants to go beyond wealth to one that can enjoy it."

- ***Dr. JC Doornick***, *aka "Dragon" Host of Rise Up With Dragon Podcast, Entrepreneur, Author, Health Transformation Coach and Kind Human*

"As an everyday bootstrap entrepreneur of over 25 years, I always struggled to find lasting peace in my business or in wanting to exit my business. I have learned much about 'exiting without exiting,' and I have The Real Jason Duncan to thank for that. It is possible to own a business without the business owning you, but in my case, only if you live by Jason's advice will you find it in between the covers of this book. Do yourself a favor and learn from a master of business in how to figure out how to live the exit lifestyle while maintaining ownership of your business."

- ***Stephen Scoggins***, *Founder/CEO of Scoggins International Inc., Serial 8 Figure Entrepreneur*

EXIT WITHOUT EXITING

HOW TO EXIT YOUR BUSINESS WITHOUT SELLING IT ... AND BEGIN LIVING THE EXIT LIFESTYLE MUCH SOONER THAN YOU EVER THOUGHT POSSIBLE

By The Real Jason Duncan

Exit Without Exiting

Published by 2 Market Media with The Real Jason Duncan.

ISBN: 979-8-218-14415-9 (PB)

This book is dedicated to my amazing team at Energy Lighting Services, who helped me build a very successful company, and then were the willing, patient, and understanding guinea pigs as I tried to implement this new idea I call exit without exiting. Without you, I would never have been able to write this book.

Thank you for being rock stars.

CONTENTS

FOREWORD

Jason Duncan is the expert in guiding entrepreneurs to escape the daily grind of business operations and attain true success. When I initially encountered Jason, I was managing multiple businesses generating six and seven-figure revenues. Like many entrepreneurs, I had experienced the ups and downs of ownership but felt confident in my ability to run a successful business. However, Jason helped me understand that there was a better approach to business that would provide the freedom and prosperity I desired.

Jason's concept of "The Ironic Prison of Entrepreneurship" was a wake-up call for me, revealing that the very businesses I had started to gain freedom were actually trapping me in a job with longer hours and increased stress. This is a common experience for entrepreneurs, who often sacrifice their time and energy on a multitude of tasks, from employee management to marketing strategies.

This book, *Exit Without Exiting: How to Exit Your Business without Selling It and Begin Living the Exit Lifestyle Much Sooner than You Ever Thought Possible*, offers a solution to this all-too-familiar struggle. It provides a roadmap to reclaiming your time and freedom, by teaching you the strategies and tools needed to run your business efficiently and effectively in fewer hours per week.
Jason is passionate about helping entrepreneurs achieve the "Exit Lifestyle" and live a life of purpose and legacy, free from the constraints of daily business operations. Following the principles outlined in this book has allowed me to do just that, and I have no doubt it can do the same for you.

So, if you're ready to escape the "Ironic Prison of Entrepreneurship" and live the life of your dreams, go ahead and turn to chapter 1 and let Jason guide you on your journey.

Dr. Justin Moseley
"The Mindset Doctor", TEDx Speaker, High Performance Coach, and Host of The Mindset Doctor Podcast

INTRODUCTION

MY VISION IS TO SEE 100,000 ENTREPRENEURS SET FREE FROM THE IRONIC PRISON OF ENTREPRENEURSHIP.

– *THE REAL JASON DUNCAN*

Your business is not delivering the results you want. You can see the gap between what you envisioned and what's actually happening. You wanted freedom and control over your time and money, but the reality is that your business now takes up all of your time and doesn't throw off the kind of money you thought it would, in order to make you financially free. Whether or not you are hitting the goals of the company, you certainly aren't hitting the goals you had for your life as an entrepreneur.

You're not alone. Hundreds of thousands of entrepreneurs just like you are trapped in the prison of entrepreneurship.

You didn't start your business to have a better job; you started it to have a better life. Yet ironically, your business is just another job for you. It's probably a better one than you had before you took the leap into business ownership, but it's still a job nonetheless. I find it sad that many business owners never experience the true freedom that entrepreneurship promises. Rather than more time and money, most end up with less time than ever before and the money doesn't usually pan out like it was *supposed to.*

In this book, you are going to learn the clear process that will help fill the gap between your experience as an entrepreneur and your ultimate desire for a certain kind of lifestyle as an entrepreneur. Unlike coaches who just help you get started or show you how to scale, I'll help you figure out how to live your ideal life while maintaining ownership of your business. This will give you the best of both worlds – a profitable and growing business, as well as the ability to live your ideal lifestyle without the need to put in insane hours and stay in the weeds every day.

The method is called **"EXIT WITHOUT EXITING."**

The result is called **"THE EXIT LIFESTYLE."**

Sidenote: If you feel compelled, please use the hashtags #ExitWithoutExiting and #TheExitLifestyle on your social media channels when sharing your reactions, perspectives, and responses to this book and the concepts I talk about within its pages. If you do a quick search on LinkedIn, Instagram, and YouTube, you will find hundreds (possibly thousands) of posts my clients and I have shared over the past few years on the topics covered here. You can find me through any of these platforms: @TheRealJasonDuncan.

You're going to learn the secrets to true delegation, and you'll finally understand what is causing all of your stress and how to eliminate it forever. With the tools and tactics you will learn here, you'll be able to build systems to help your team qualify, prospect, sell, and close more deals and ultimately drive long-term predictable revenue. Not only that, but you will learn some proven strategies used by millionaires to find, hire, onboard, and train rockstar employees who will help your business thrive in your absence. Again, this book will set you out on the path to finding freedom from the ironic prison of entrepreneurship. Many people say that entrepreneurship is like building a plane in flight. That's a pretty good analogy, but with this book, you have someone who's an expert in aeronautical engineering with you.

Most people start from where they are today and work forward, but that's the wrong way to build a business. You need to work backwards and start with the end in mind. What lifestyle do you truly desire? Let's start there and build a business that supports that, rather than building your life around the business. You're not going to make great leaps in one step, but you can cover much more ground faster if you start with the end in mind.

I believe that business ownership is not the goal; rather, it should provide the financial resources to support your family and personal life outside the business. That's the goal--gaining the resources to have the lifestyle you want to live. But so many entrepreneurs just like you build their lives around their businesses. They live off of the leftovers after the business is done with them, and that's the wrong way to do it. I believe this, because I am certain you started your business in order to give yourself a better life, not just to give you a better job. That is why I wrote this book. I want to teach you how to design your business around your life, rather than your life being built around your business. I want to take you from being an owner-operator to becoming an owner-investor.

I've helped founders just like you free up over 50% of their time with the four core principles that you will learn in this book. Instead of being in the weeds 40 to 80 hours a week, they now are able to focus on more important tasks in the business, or spend more time with their families. Frankly, the concepts I'm going to share with you will allow you to run your business in as little as 10 hours a week. If you could begin living this way without having to sell your business like I've helped so many other people do – if you could exit without exiting--what would stop you from achieving that?

What exactly is the exit lifestyle, you ask? I'll explain that in more detail throughout the book, and especially in Chapter 2.

Whether you have just started your business, you're in the middle of it, or you have been running it for over a decade, you should have one goal – to create a business that generates enough cash for you to live a financially free life, without having to work like crazy to sustain it. When your business is operating like this, it means you have been successful in maintaining SCALE. More importantly, it means you now have **options**. You have the option to start another division of your company, sell your company, step away from day-to-day operations, travel more, or even start a new business that excites your passions.

You might want to sell or "exit" your business the traditional way, or you might prefer to build a legacy. I don't judge which option you choose---what I judge is if you think being in the weeds is the only way to create success. This means you have not figured out a way to live the exit lifestyle, and you're just hoping that someday in the future, you can sell the business and finally be able to enjoy life.

But you don't have to wait!

As an entrepreneur, I've made many mistakes in my business. I didn't set up my business correctly, I had a partnership issue that almost bankrupted me. You name it. However true, you can learn from my mistakes and use my experiences to rise up in the ranks and have a business you enjoy much faster.

One of my gifts is teaching. I love teaching, and I'm good at it. I can explain complex concepts that help give people comprehension and understanding. I have a masters in education, as well as a bachelor's in ministry. I spent 13 years in pastoral ministry and four years as a school teacher before I became an "accidental entrepreneur." Since 2010, the businesses I've launched have been featured in several publications, including the *Inc.* 5000 list as one of the fastest-growing privately held companies in America and one of *Entrepreneur* magazine's top entrepreneurial companies in America. I have founded 12 companies that are involved in everything from e-commerce, to consulting services, to real estate holdings. And as far as I know, I'm the first millionaire in my family.

Since I exited my business without selling it in 2020–what I call "exit without exiting"–I've been blessed to work directly with hundreds of business owners to show each of them their own pathways to freedom as entrepreneurs. I've been able to use my gifts of teaching and leadership, along with my track record as a successful entrepreneur, to help thousands of entrepreneurs through my coaching platform, my online courses, my keynote speeches, my podcast, and my mastermind. I hope to help millions more with this book. Let's get to how you too can "exit without exiting" so you can begin living the exit lifestyle.

1. WHAT DOES IT MEAN TO EXIT YOUR BUSINESS?

EDWARD'S STORY

Edward is your typical entrepreneur. He spent an entire decade building his business from the ground up. No franchise. No pre-built systems. No established customer base. Nothing. It was simply a dream and a willingness to see it come to life. In the beginning, Edward simply had the goal of building a business that would pay the bills and maybe provide him with some freedom of time that his old life in corporate America never seemed to offer.

For ten years, he poured his life into creating this business with his own bare hands. His blood, sweat, and tears had gone into it in order for the business to become the best it could possibly be. Edward had built a great team around him, and they were growing their revenue slowly each year. They were selling fantastic products and services to their loyal customer base, which Edward felt really good about. It was so fulfilling to know that the company he started from absolutely nothing was providing such great service to so many people. He had spent many long weeks building up this business, putting his heart, time, and full energy into making it succeed.

It was not uncommon for Edward to work 60, 70, or 80 hours per week and sometimes even up to 100 when a big project was on the line. Oftentimes, Edward would feel compelled to miss family functions or big events that were important to those he loved. This always bothered him, but he assumed it was required of every entrepreneur. After all, the social media gurus all talked about hustling and grinding. According to those Lamborghini-driving influencers, he was supposed to be working like a dog in hopes that one day someone would swoop in and write him a huge check for his company, and he'd finally be free.

Over time, this started to eat away at Edward's emotions more and more. He had missed more of his daughter's dance recitals than he'd care to admit, more than a few of his son's soccer games, and he even missed one big family reunion that he didn't remember was happening at the time. His wife was always very supportive, because she also believed that what he was doing was somehow normal for entrepreneurs. And she knew that his work was very important to him. Even still, it was very difficult to have him absent for so many of life's big events. She understood the bigger picture – at least that's what she thought – although it often caused some distress to their family. She was never hateful, and she never nagged him about all of the hours he continued to put in at the office. It was his business after all, and she understood the significance of his hard work. If he didn't work, they wouldn't be able to pay the bills.

Then, it happened. Edward decided enough was enough and it was time to sell the business. It was time to exit. It was time to cash in on all his hard work and finally begin experiencing the freedom that he set out to achieve as his ultimate goal 10 years ago when he started the business. He was generating around $4-5 million a year in revenue with an 8% net margin, and he was taking home around $300,000 in personal income. Not too shabby, considering he had only been making $90,000 a year as a regional manager at his corporate job a decade ago. But the business had about $750,000 in debt. He leased his office space and held very little inventory.

Edward soon found out that even though he had good revenue numbers and a decent bottom line, buyers weren't flocking to him as he'd expected. The broker he hired to help him sell the business wasn't much help. Each time a potential buyer took a look at the offer memorandum, they would ask a few questions and never call back. Eventually, someone came along who seemed promising and legitimately interested. At long last, Edward and his broker met with a potential buyer.

That meeting changed everything for Edward.

The potential buyer explained that while he was indeed interested in Edward's business, he was concerned that the business seemed to revolve around Edward: his skills, his contacts, his abilities, his ideas, his personality. Everything in the business somehow went back to Edward. As it turned out, this was the reason so many buyers had expressed initial interest but then backed away. They knew that if they bought the business and Edward wasn't involved, the revenue would tank. That's not a good investment for any buyer.

This was a huge blow to Edward. All this time, he believed that if he hustled and put in the time to build a business, he'd eventually be able to exit it and be financially free. Sadly, that simply wasn't true.

The reality slowly set in with Edward. There was no quick way out of his business that would lead to financial freedom. He had built it the wrong way. He was going to either have to stay in it and run it until he was unable to, or he was going to have to sell it for pennies on the dollar as compared to what he thought it was worth. Neither option seemed good to him.

After a few months of negotiating with the only potential buyer who returned the broker's calls, Edward found himself sitting at the closing table ready to receive a check. Someone else was about to take over and buy his business from him – the one he spent years of his life building up. The check wasn't as big as he'd once thought it should have been, but there really wasn't any other option. Sure, he could have kept grinding away at it himself, but he was tired and ready to move on.

When he started 10 years ago, he knew that he'd eventually want to step out of the daily grind. He was working so many hours, which realistically was only viable for a certain amount of time before he'd burn out completely. It was always the goal to work hard now for a payoff later, but was this the exit he truly wanted? No.

The buyer made it clear that the only way he would buy the business was if Edward remained on as CEO for three years to ensure a smooth transition to the new ownership group and help maintain revenue and profitability. Edward would get a check at closing for half of the agreed-upon sale price and the other half would have to be earned by Edward over the next three years. Assuming that revenue goals were hit and the profitability remained the same, Edward would get the second half of the purchase price – even though the total amount was much less than what he truly wanted. This exit wasn't going to be quick. He had to earn his way out.

As Edward sat at the closing table, thoughts raced through his mind about this sale and how it would forever change his life but not the way he originally thought it would. He had a lot of mixed emotions. He'd truly thrown himself into his business in order to make it succeed day in and day out. He'd become so used to his routine of running his company and being the one final decision-maker on everything, he wasn't sure what being an employee was going to feel like. It had been ten years since he'd had a boss. He thought to himself: *Is this what an exit is really all about? Is my exit really this lackluster? This isn't what I thought it would be. Where did I go wrong?*

Of course, this was his only real option. At least now, his 70 and 80-hour workweeks would be cut back a bit, and there was a light at the end of the tunnel. His continued presence in the business would hopefully ensure and maintain the company's profitability, and he'd get the other half of the money eventually. He just had to work for three more years… but now as an employee, not as the owner. This just seemed wrong to Edward.

Like many entrepreneurs, Edward's desire to sell his business conjured up images of huge checks, luxurious vacations, and fancy cars. But the reality was not so sweet. Because he'd built his business around himself, his only exit was to either shut the business down or sign up for this earnout.

Now Edward was going to have to watch someone else take over the ownership of the business that he spent 10 years of his life building. It was a difficult decision for him, especially since he was going to continue to have to work in the business – not the as the owner but as an employee. He justified to himself that this would eventually lead him to the lifestyle he truly desired. "Just a little while longer," he thought to himself.

But for now, and for the next three years, he would be an employee of the business he started. As CEO, he was going to have to manage daily, weekly, monthly, and quarterly tasks to make sure that revenue targets were hit. If he didn't hit these revenue targets, the other half of his payout in the sale would not happen. The exit lifestyle was still three years away for Edward. Freedom was still not a reality, because he would have to remain trapped by this business.

While Edward felt thankful that he could sell the business, he also wished there was a way for him to have a clean break. Instead of keeping a foot in the door, he would rather simply accept the check and walk away. Unfortunately for him, Edward built a business that relied too much on him as the owner. The new buyers needed his input and his expertise in order to make the business work. The pressure was on him to bring them profitability and continue to grow revenue.

Edward knew that he was a key factor in its success; he had come to terms with the notion that he'd have to stick around for a while. It almost seemed unfair to him that it was still his responsibility to continue the success of the buyer. Why did he have to make sure that the business he no longer owned was running correctly and profitably? Why was he responsible for the success of the newcomers? The Instagram gurus never talked about this.

Edward also contemplated the fact that at this point in his life, this check from the sale was not enough money to never work again. Even though the sale would provide him with a large lump sum of money – enough to help him slow down and work a little less, start living his life more fully and invest more time into his family, enjoy his hobbies and other activities – it wasn't enough to do nothing for the rest of his life. The worst part was that without the second half of the payout, he would likely have to work full-time at something for many years.

Was it all worth it? Had he made the right choices? Was there a way that he could have built his business to run without him, or did he make himself too indisposable? What would the sale have been like if he had built a business that didn't require him so much? What could he have done differently?

CHERYL'S STORY

Cheryl is sitting at the closing table of a venture capital firm in a tall, glass-covered building in the city. This VC firm is about to write her a check that will change the course of her life forever. Unlike the check that Edward received at his closing, this check was the kind of money that would give Cheryl financial independence for as long as she lived. Never again would Cheryl have to work; her days of sitting in the office and taking on the daily grind were completely over. This was the kind of buyout that creates generational wealth; this was the exit that every entrepreneur dreams of attaining.

Ten years ago at her daughter's 9th birthday party, Cheryl's friend Diane pulled up in a brand new Range Rover. While Cheryl was impressed with the new car, she wondered how Diane had been able to afford it. They weren't extremely close friends and hadn't seen each other in several months, but Cheryl was pretty sure that Diane and her husband couldn't really afford a luxury like this. As she recalled, Diane's husband owned a small home service business and Diane was the office manager. She thought to herself, "*They don't make that much money, do they?*" Diane's daughter lept from the back seat to greet Cheryl's daughter and her friends, the girls squealed at one another, hugged and then ran off to enjoy the party. Cheryl said how great it was to see her and made a comment about how nice the new SUV was. Diane explained that her husband had just sold their business and this new ride was something Diane had always wanted. After a few minutes of chatting, the ladies went to enjoy the birthday party with the kids.

For a solid week after the party, Cheryl couldn't get that new Range Rover and Diane's story about their experience selling their business off of her mind. Cheryl worked part-time as a bank teller, and her husband was a plant manager at a local manufacturing facility. They were comfortable and had all the necessities any family of four living in the midwest could want. Cheryl's job allowed her plenty of time to take the kids to school, pick them up and take them to their activities. It was something that she and her husband really wanted for their family. But her aging minivan started to look dull compared to Diane's new Range Rover. "*What if I started a business?*" she thought to herself.

As you can tell from the way Cheryl's story started here in the book, she did in fact start a business. Her venture went very well for her financially. The mail order business that she started in her kitchen turned into a full-fledged ecommerce business that brought it millions annually in recurring revenue. Her husband stayed on at the plant to keep their health insurance, but he had to change his work hours to take the kids to and from school and their activities because Cheryl became busier and busier as the business grew. Unfortunately, she couldn't act as the family manager she once was.

Cheryl spent a little more than 10 years of her life building this business. Unlike Edward, her business was created so that it didn't require her to be at the center of everything. She was pretty good at putting systems and people into place so that the business could run without her involved in every decision. Nevertheless, Cheryl regularly put in 100 hour weeks. Why? Because her goal was to have the ultimate multi-million dollar exit that so many entrepreneurs dream of. She wanted to buy a new Range Rover some day...one just like Diane had. This was her driving motivation to spend so many hours each day in her business.

She knew that if she built her business the right way, someone would offer her an ungodly amount of money at some point. She didn't take much income out of the business for her salary as it continued to grow. She figured that entrepreneurs were supposed to reinvest profits and pay themselves a meager income, so she only pulled out the equivalent of what she used to make at the bank. She figured that if she maintained a modest lifestyle now and kept reinvesting profits into the business, eventually she could sell it for a lot of money. Cheryl's problem was that she built her life around the business, rather than the business around her life. She worked so much that there became very little time left over to experience life.

Cheryl was able to establish systems and processes and invest in the right people so that her business ran like a well-oiled machine. Even though she was rarely away from the office, she was confident that she could spend time away from the business without it suffering if she wanted to. But at the end of the day, Cheryl was married to her work. She couldn't see past the daily grind of business ownership to realize that the lifestyle she truly wanted – and thought could only happen after she sold the business – was available for her now. She didn't have to wait for an eventual sale.

Cheryl sat at the closing table ready to receive a check from a buyer that would change her life forever. Finally, she could begin living life on her own terms. She had spent 10 years building this business. Her oldest daughter was about to go to start her sophomore year in college, and her son was starting his senior year in high school. She wondered, *"Where did the time go?"* She had missed many volleyball matches and football games during the pursuit of building a business that she could eventually sell. It was finally about to happen. Today was her big day. After today, she would be able to spend all the time she ever wanted with her kids and her husband. But in that moment of contemplation, she realized that the money she was about to get was not a fair exchange for the time she missed with her kids during their teenage years. She saw it in her husband's eyes, as he sat next to her, holding her hand. There was a sense of sorrow that she didn't expect. Cheryl perceived that he also knew that the ten years of building a business for this multimillion-dollar exit now seemed a bit unsatisfying, compared to the years she could have spent paying more attention to her family.

She was going to walk away with more money than she ever could spend in her lifetime. She had often thought to herself: *I'm doing this for my family. I'm preparing them for a better life…one I never had. They won't ever have to drive my grandkids around in an old minivan.* She always knew that she could make it as an entrepreneur. Even though she felt sorrow for the time lost, the best part about this exit for Cheryl was that it would give her the freedom to do whatever she wanted. Other than the short transition period that the new owners required to get organized and up and running, she didn't have to stick around for years like Edward did. Her ties were completely cut, and she was ready to move on with her life.

When it was time to sign the paperwork and give everything over to the new owners, Cheryl was happy, even if a bit unsatisfied.

She knew that in a few weeks when the transition was complete and the new ownership was in place, she was free. She would spend the next six months traveling around the world with her friends and family members that she'd missed so much time with. She was able to attend her son's football games and talked to her daughter about college life from time to time. She began realizing even more deeply how much she had missed of their lives over the past decade.

In contrast to Edward, Cheryl was fully able to enjoy the exit lifestyle now that she had exited her business. Her total exit and the money she received afforded her that privilege. But both of them lost time with the ones they loved in pursuit of building their businesses. At the end of the day, both Edward and Cheryl had regrets about the choices they had made that stole precious time from their personal lives. Both of them were able to sell their companies; both of them had been working terribly long hours for a decade in order to succeed; both of them missed family functions; both of them worked incredibly hard at the expense of other aspects of their lives. The biggest difference is that Edward didn't embrace delegation, establish systems, or invest in people, causing him to have to sell his business through an earnout. Cheryl, on the other hand, was able to fully exit and walk away because she embraced delegation, established the right systems and processes, and invested in her people. But at the end of the day, they both traded time for money. They both missed a decade of their ideal lifestyles in pursuit of building a business, hoping that one day it would "all be worth it." They didn't start with the end in mind.

TIME VS MONEY

I believe that most entrepreneurs like Edward and Cheryl leverage time for money, but this is the exact opposite of what they should be doing.

Many entrepreneurs speak disparagingly about W2 earners and

talk about how they trade an hour for a dollar amount. The sad but honest truth is that while entrepreneurs don't generally get paid an hourly wage, they are still trading time for money in most cases. There's not a lot of difference between hourly workers and business owners when it comes to the money-for-time conversation. But it doesn't have to be that way. The beauty of entrepreneurship is the promise of time – time to do what you want, when you want, with whom you want. Time is the thing that entrepreneurship should get you the most of.

Think about this for a minute: money is a renewable resource. You can get more of it after you spend it. (That doesn't mean it's easy, but you certainly can get more.) But time is non-renewable. You can never get time back. Both Cheryl & Edward leveraged their time for money, and at the end of the day the thing they both regretted most was the time they missed with their families. Had they leveraged money for time, they both would have had totally different endings to their stories.

One of the methods I teach my clients is something called the 10-Block Weekly Scheduling Method that will free up more than half of your time each week while still getting the same amount of tasks completed. This method is successful because it is "focus management" instead of time management. Time management is a myth. Time cannot be managed any more than I can go down to the river and manage the flow of the water with my hands. Time keeps marching on, no matter what. We simply cannot manage time… but we CAN manage our focus.

My clients who implement this 10-Block Weekly Scheduling Method tell me how much stress it takes out of their lives, because now they're not running around like a chicken with their head cut off and doing whatever is urgent at the moment. That's one of the common outcomes of modern time management techniques: it keeps us busy, and we end up doing what is urgent rather than what is important. People who manage their focus with tools like the one I created learn to stay focused and not allow interruptions to derail their productivity. Perhaps if Cheryl & Edward had used a similar tool in their businesses, their exits would have ended up much more satisfying. (You will read more about the 10-Block Weekly Scheduling Method in James' story in the next chapter.)

TWO DIFFERENT TYPES OF EXITS

Edward & Cheryl both exited their companies, but in different ways. The problem is that most entrepreneurs think that every exit is just like Cheryl's. If you just work hard enough and long enough, someday there will be somebody who will swoop in and give you more money than you could ever spend in a lifetime. That's when you'll finally be free and able to live the exit lifestyle. This is referred to as a "total exit."

Unfortunately, that's a very naive assumption and not necessarily the only way to exit a business. Remember Edward? He assumed his exit would be like Cheryl's too, but it didn't happen. Most people perceive the term *exiting* as a complete financial and physical exit. It's a full-on walk away, where you're selling the business and never having to return again. You're done. You've paid your dues and put in your time. Now you can wash your hands clean and live a lifestyle of your choosing. Yes, it does happen sometimes, but not often. Cheryl's story is literally one-in-a-million, and most entrepreneurs never experience that same outcome.

Let's look back at Edward for a minute. His exit was just a financial exit and not a complete, physical exit. That's what we call an "earnout," which happens when you sell your business and "earn out" the money that was agreed upon in the purchase agreement over time. This could be two years, or it could be ten years. You essentially have to earn your way out, whatever the time commitment may be.

Here's an example of how an earnout works. Let's say you agreed to sell your business to a willing buyer for $1,000,000. The buyer may give you $500,000 today and $100,000 every year over the course of five years. However, this only happens for as long as the business meets the agreed-upon profitability or revenue targets. In this way, you are earning the sale price over time *after the sale.* That was Edward's story… he had to earn his way out.

If you're like most entrepreneurs, you think that the two ways illustrated in Cheryl's and Edward's stories are the only two ways to exit a business. Well, surprise! There's actually a third way – one that lets you leverage money for time and allows you to live the exit lifestyle today without necessarily selling your business.

This is the core concept of what I'm going to show you in the pages of this book. You can, in fact, exit your business without exiting. That's right! You can begin living the exit lifestyle without having to sell your business. You don't have to wait for the multimillion-dollar exit that Cheryl experienced, and you don't have to go through the pain of an earnout like Edward did.

There is a way to give yourself the exit lifestyle that neither Cheryl nor Edward were able to achieve until after they had sold their businesses to someone else. And for Edward, it took even longer because of the earnout period. This third way is completely different, which is something that I like to call *"exit without exiting."* This means you're able to leave the daily operations of your business without selling it.

This book will teach you exactly how to pull this off… but first, let's address an important question.

WHY DO WE NEED TO EXIT IN THE FIRST PLACE?

One of the questions that I'm always asked is: *Why do I need or want to exit?* One of the main reasons is that this helps you protect the value of the business that you have built over the years. According to most mergers-and-acquisitions experts, when the business owner is critical to the day-to-day operations, the valuation of that business drops by 30 to 50%. Therefore, building a business that does not require you to be involved in the daily operations will increase the value of your company significantly. This is why it's important to learn how to exit the daily operations of your business.

Sometimes a business owner can become physically unable to keep up with the demands of running his business. It's grown too much over time, and it's become too much of a burden. When this happens, the business value will slowly decrease over time because of his inability to keep up. For example, if you open an electrical contracting company and you're the main electrician, you will eventually have to find someone else to work with before you get into your early 60s. Why? Because at that point, you won't be able to keep up with the demand of the business that you've grown. Your knees won't work as well, your back may be weak, and you probably won't be able to crawl around in those tight spaces like you once could. You're the number one guy, so it's all resting on you. So it makes sense that your business value would go down simply because you can't work as much as you could when you were younger. This happens with a lot of businesses when the head honcho ends up needing to exit because it's become too much. At that point, the owner assumes he has a valuable asset in the business itself, but that asset could have decreased in value over time significantly. In reality, it's not positive for the value if the biggest asset of the business is the owner.

The circumstance is the same if the owner's mental capacity suddenly changes. While this is not as common as a decline in physical capacity, mental capacity decline does happen from time to time. Sometimes, owners begin losing memory as they grow older. Brain fog and cognitive decline prevent them from being as sharp as they once were. Suppose this owner is the lynchpin to the daily operations of the business. In that case, the value of that business will drop significantly over time if someone else doesn't step in and take control for the owner who's not able to perform like he used to.

Consider the private pilot who's spent a career flying executives around the world. Once he's over 40, he has to start renewing his medical certificate every two years. An aviation medical examiner (AME) will test several things. His distance vision must be 20/40 or better in each eye, with or without correction. His near vision has to be 20/40 or better in each eye, as measured at 16 inches. Generally speaking, by the age of 65, he's not going to be able to maintain his pilot's license for commercial flying, which means he has to give up his wings to someone younger. And if he has built a business that relied on his ability to fly executives, his business is now in severe trouble and in danger of being worthless.

So the question remains: *Why do we need to exit?*

First of all, it helps you protect the value of the businesses that you've been building for years. If your abilities – physical, mental, or otherwise – prevent you from continuing to operate the business or to grow the business, preparing to exit the daily operations of the business will save it from a severe decline in value. Sometimes, it's necessary to exit so that the inevitable doesn't happen.

Another reason to exit is because you may eventually start to desire another type of lifestyle. Maybe your passions, desires, and dreams are no longer lining up with the business that you started long ago. Maybe you've been running that business forever and feel ready to have freedom for travel, other hobbies, or your family. Sometimes, exiting the business is the best way to achieve the lifestyle that you're wanting to live.

Let's look at the pros and cons of the two ways to exit, as illustrated by Edward and Cheryl. You have the "total exit" and the "earnout." As we've discussed, the total exit is both financial and physical. The earnout is a financial exit only, but you are still physically required to stay in the business for a time.

	The Earnout	The Total Exit
PROS	• These types of transactions are typically more common and easier to manage. • They don't take as long to execute. • You will end up having influence after you've technically sold the business to another owner. • It allows you to protect your baby from going in the wrong direction. • You get a lump sum at the beginning. That liquidity can help cushion you and give you the opportunity to do something new if you want to.	• It generates new and great liquidity for you at the sale. • It allows you to break free from your business and pursue other things immediately. • It gives you the ability to diversify your personal finances rather than having 100% of your largest investment tied up in one business.
CONS	• You have to stay in the business after you've sold it. • Now, you're actually just an employee. • It's generally not going to get you as much cash as you would if you did a total exit. • You have to wait a long time to get your money. • If the business doesn't meet certain milestones for any reason, you may not ever get the other portion of the money that you were supposed to get during the earnout period. • It prevents you from going on to your next adventure until after the earnout period.	• You're going to be completely disconnected from any decision-making power of the business moving forward. • It can be hard to watch your baby change with new ownership. • A total exit is sometimes a highly complex transaction that will require extensive negotiations over a lengthy time frame. • The sale agreements on these types of exits are expensive and require a lot of due diligence. • You might have to sign a non-compete.

Which type of exit are you considering for your business? Remember, there is a third alternative to these types of exits, and one that you may find much more attractive.

2. WHAT IS THE EXIT LIFESTYLE?

JAMES'S STORY

James is an entrepreneur who started a business about five years ago. His story is going to become a recurring theme throughout this book, because he took a different path when it came to his exit. His path led him to the exit lifestyle much sooner and without all of the regrets over lost time that plagued both Edward and Cheryl. Rather than seeking a total exit or even looking for an earnout, the method James chose to exit his business is what I call "exit without exiting." Because of his commitment to four core principles – which I share in Chapters 6 through 9 – he was able to begin living the exit lifestyle much sooner than Cheryl and Edward. And he didn't have to miss any soccer games or dance recitals along the way.

Before I go into all the details about James and how he did what he did, I promised you in Chapter 1 that I would explain what the exit lifestyle is. So, allow me to do that here.

It's the lifestyle you will live after you have exited your business and the need to earn money is no longer a primary concern for you and your family. It doesn't necessarily mean total financial independence, but it does mean that you will no longer have to trade time for money. It's about living the life you truly desire, rather than living the life that your business allows.

The exit lifestyle is very different from person to person. Some will want to travel to exotic locations around the world after they exit. Others will simply want to spend more time with their friends and family. Some will want to throw their energy and time into mission work or volunteer opportunities. Still others will want to start a new business in a field that closely aligns with their passions and desires.

The exit lifestyle is not a singular concept. It is not defined only by luxury items, expensive vacations, or fancy new Range Rovers. It is different for everyone.

It boils down to two words: *choice & control.* This lifestyle is about having the ability to make the choice each day over what activities you're going to invest your time into. It's about having the control to make decisions without the fear of your business or income failing.

When you have full control over the choices you make each day without fear of loss, you have achieved "the exit lifestyle." And you do not have to sell your business in order to attain it.

You are an above average person. (Otherwise, you wouldn't be reading this book!) As such, you can probably already see that the exit lifestyle is not destined only for people like Cheryl, who walk away from a closing table at a VC firm with a huge lump sum of cash. Nor is it a lifestyle popularized by Instagram influencers who flex by sitting on the hoods of their new Mclarens and G Wagons. True, that is a *version* of the exit lifestyle, but it isn't the *definition.*

Think about it this way. If you DID sell your business for $100 million and never had to work again, what would you do each day? Whatever that is, you have the choice and control to make that decision because you are not beholden to any business that makes you trade your time for more dollars. Your lifestyle would be very different from the 60, 70, 80 hour workweeks you're used to as an entrepreneur.

But what if I told you that the exit lifestyle is not something you have to wait to enjoy? What if you can attain it now without working insane hours and having to wait for a magical VC genie to offer you three wishes? You certainly don't have to transition from owner to employee in your business for five years before you can begin enjoying the exit lifestyle.

James is not sitting at a closing table. He's not about to receive a check that will change his life. He's not even going to receive a check that will change his next three years. James isn't getting a large lump sum of money like Edward or Cheryl. Instead, James has been getting checks on every single payday from the company. Every two weeks, just like clockwork, James gets paid. His controller initiates the payroll direct deposit just like she does for all of James' 15 employees. And let's be honest – he's making really good money. His business is currently generating about $7 million in annual revenue. As the founder of a successful, privately held company, his personal income is somewhere between $500,000 and $700,000, depending upon the year. Yes, his payroll checks are much smaller than that. The direct deposits he receives every two weeks are usually around $8,000 to $10,000. The rest of his income is distributed on a quarterly or annual basis, according to the business profitability. As of today, the company is continuing to prove itself as a very profitable company. It's netting about 12% and continuing to grow year over year.

Like both Edward and Cheryl, James built his business from the ground up, but he's done it the right way. Of course, for the first year or so, he worked very long hours-sometimes up to 80 or 90 hours per week. He was the chief of everything when he started. He did all the sales, all the correspondence, all the design work, and even the administrative tasks. But James knew that was not a sustainable model. During the course of those first two years, he began delegating tasks and responsibilities as often as he could.

He knew that he had to hire good team members whom he could trust. He began to see the value in investing in them, training them, buying them all the software that they needed, and then implementing systems and processes. He recognized early on how negative that stress would impact the growth of his business, so he made sure to reduce and eliminate it as much as possible – not only from his own life, but from the lives of his employees as well. James learned that he did not have to be the hero of the business; in order to grow, he had to let other people take on responsibilities and tasks instead of doing everything himself.

EXIT WITHOUT EXITING

After five years as the owner-operator and CEO of his business, he made the decision that he'd like to pursue other opportunities and passions. James began the transition from owner-operator to owner-investor. For the past two years, he'd only been coming to the office three days a week. His leadership team has been firmly in charge of the daily operations, and he was confident in their decision-making skills. As a matter of fact, on more than one occasion they had implemented new systems that grew revenue and profits in a notable way without direct input from James. His primary role was setting the vision and communicating it clearly to his team on a regular basis. And since he was not embroiled in the weeds of daily operations for the last two years, he spent his time building the assets of the business. He purchased a building and some land and then moved the business out of the leased complex they had occupied before. Next, he worked with a software company to develop an app for his sales team to use in order to close deals faster while in the field. He had even worked with a trademark attorney to get his intellectual property protected. James had built a great company that was now an extremely valuable asset. For him, it was time to exit but not to sell. No, he simply wanted to step away from the day-to-day operations. He was ready to "exit without exiting."

Unlike Edward and Cheryl, James had built his business in a

way that didn't rely on him to be the hero. Therefore, he hadn't missed time with his family over the past five years while he was growing his business. He coached the lacrosse team of his oldest son and was always present at his daughter's recitals. His wife enjoyed the income that the business provided for the family, but more than that, she was happy that James was always available if they needed him.

Today, his leadership team is sitting at the conference table for their monthly leadership team check-in meeting. James has told them ahead of time that he has something special to announce. This is not the closing table that Cheryl and Edward experienced. This is just a normal conference room table where his leadership team sits to discuss business operations – it's where he meets with them once a month to make sure all is well. Today though, it is serving as the place where James will announce his big transition.

After complimenting his team on their tremendous results and recounting some great stories of success and failure over the past five years, James reveals: "I have decided to move out of the CEO role, but don't worry! I'm not selling the company." While everyone appeared a bit perplexed, they were not worried. After all, he was not really involved in the daily operations anymore, and they were completely comfortable with their roles as department heads. James continued, "I plan to promote each of you from department heads to vice presidents. You will now be even more integral at the forefront of the company, and you will continue to run the daily operations of the business. But now, I will only be checking in with you all once a quarter. Just like you run your weekly meetings without me, you will now run the monthly check-ins without me as well. You and I will meet once a quarter. I will review financials, of course, and make sure you continue to have the resources available for you to succeed and continue to grow the business, but I will not be involved in the execution of the strategies to realize the vision I've set. You have proven to be faithful and loyal leaders in the company, and I trust you. In exchange for your new responsibility and titles, you are all getting a raise." The perplexed looks were slowly turning into big, proud grins. As James surveyed the room, he looked deeply into the eyes of his leadership team and was overcome with joy. He had built this. He had created an atmosphere where these amazing people could rise up and lead his company – his baby – without him looking over their shoulders. He was about to exit, and it was exciting!

It's worth noting that the raise each new VP was getting was not adding to the P&L. Rather he planned to give part of his salary to each of his leaders, dividing it between them. In this way, they would understand that he was truly investing in them and not adding a burdensome increase to the monthly budget of the company. Just like any other investment, this would initially take money out of James' pocket. Eventually though, he knew this investment in his people would bring a large return to his personal bottom line. Essentially, that's what all investments are supposed to do, and that's the type of investment that James decided to make in his people.

His plan was set. Each quarter moving forward, he told them that he would come in and have a two-hour meeting with his leadership team in order to review financial objectives and make sure that everything was running smoothly. For the first six months, he would be checking in individually with each VP on a monthly basis just to make sure that all of the operations were completely in line with his vision. After that period of transition, James would then only be checking in once a quarter. Of course, he would continue to be available by phone, text, email, or through the internal channels that they had built within the company in order to communicate easily. But now was going to be his time to exit without exiting – James decided that he wants to move on to something different.

For a very long time, James had aspirations of starting another business, though he simply never had the time to do so. His first business had been a resounding success, but his interests had changed. Like most people, as you get exposed to new ideas and experiences, your desires change. Sure, James enjoyed his business.

He loved his employees immensely. But the core business itself was no longer fulfilling. Most entrepreneurs would look to exit at this point, sell it to a third party, or take a lump sum of cash and move on. The total exit was an option for James. His business was likely worth 6 to 8 times EBITDA, which would net him millions of dollars. The downside to this though – as outlined at the end of Chapter 1 – is that James would lose control over the future of the business, including the welfare of his employees whom he loved very much. And this big payday would also get cut in half by the tax man. That just didn't seem like a good option for James.

He had an idea for a new business and one that excited him. His other business concept wasn't going to take a large financial investment to get it up and running. He knew he could easily bootstrap the new one, just as he did for this first one. Though true, he needed some time to make it all happen, and even though he had only been going into the office three days a week for a while now, that still didn't provide him with the focused time he knew he'd need to start another business. He knew that he had a good idea, but he couldn't act upon it until he was able to totally step away from the daily operations of his first business.

James was able to accomplish this and live the exit lifestyle without selling his business because he committed to four core principles that allowed him to exit without exiting. It's an unknown third option that most entrepreneurs don't really know about when they're considering exiting their business. Of course, like Cheryl, you could simply walk away, never go back, and have more money than you ever know how to spend. That all sounds great, right? Right. However true, most entrepreneurs never get to experience that kind of exit, because it's not a reality for the large majority of business owners.

Based on research, only about 2% of entrepreneurs will end up selling their business for an amount of money that would allow them to be financially independent. Most business owners simply close their businesses when they no longer are able to run them. Many that do sell will end up selling for just six or seven figures, which doesn't completely change your life. If you are one of those lucky entrepreneurs who sell it for eight or nine figures – congratulations! You have beaten the odds. Most entrepreneurs are very optimistic and do believe in that potential, but reality tells us that only a few can do it. A large sum of business owners will end up like Edward, who was able to sell the business after a decade of extremely dedicated hard work. However, now he's going to be required to stick around to ensure that he actually gets his big six-figure check. Yes, this payout will give him some freedom and allow him to go on some vacations, treat himself to something new, and not work for a little while. But that check will not change his life. As a matter of fact, he will still be stuck in the business for the next three years.

MY WAY: THE THIRD WAY

So what exactly is this third way of exiting? How can I set my business up so that I can exit without exiting? This book is going to teach you all that you need to know about setting yourself up for success. Just to review, in Chapter 1, we discussed two of the most popular ways to exit a business which are the total exit and the earnout. Edward showed us what an earnout looks like, and Cheryl illustrated a total exit. However, the third and far less common option is the *exit without exiting*. This option allows you to maintain the financial and tax benefits of business ownership, but all while having none of the operational requirements or stress. It's how James built his business and how he was able to exit the daily operations, maintain a nice income, and still have ownership. It's the best of both worlds, as this option gives you money and restores your time.

In her situation, Cheryl got both money and time, but only after she sold the business. Before she sold it, she took out a meager income and had very little time to live her life the way she ultimately wanted to live it. Although she managed to walk away in the best possible financial scenario, Cheryl is a two percenter. She's one of the extremely rare cases, and you can't bank on this happening for you. I hate to be the one to have to break the news... but the likelihood of that being you is very small. Of course, I'd love for that to be me! I'd love for that to be you, as well. Although true, speaking from reality, we have to plan for the fact that it's not going to happen this way. Not all businesses are sold for such large sums of money, but that doesn't mean there isn't a better way to do it.

Don't be like Edward, who sold the business but had to stick around for several years before he broke free. Instead, think about it this way. What if it was possible for you to exit the business without selling the business? This way, you're able to turn over the daily operations while also having time for starting something new, going on a big adventure, traveling to volunteer, doing mission work, or basically whatever it is that you want to do. When you take this third way – the exit without exiting – you get control over the choices you make each day. Choice and control. That is the core of the exit lifestyle.

MY STORY

Let's go all the way back to the beginning. When I was a kid, my dad drove an orange Volkswagen Beetle. He has a picture of me standing in the front seat of that car, holding onto the steering wheel and peeking through the windshield with a huge grin on my face. I was too young to even remember it, but my dad always told me that something about that car really made me smile. I loved the car so much that in my adulthood, I bought multiple old Volkswagen Beetles and restored several of them. I own several books about Volkswagens and have a few miniature Beetle models sitting on my bookshelf here in my office as I'm writing this. As a kid, the love affair that I had with that orange Volkswagen made me want to draw cars. I can remember being a young child and going through sheet after sheet of paper, just drawing Bugs (as they are called) repeatedly. That's one of the earliest memories I have, just sitting down, drawing cars.

We recently moved, and during the move I found a box of my old drawings, which was nostalgic for me. I even found my old art portfolio from high school, which had more than a few drawings of cars and trucks. When I was in high school, I decided that I wanted to become a car designer. I thought I'd go to art school, become an Industrial Designer, and then work for GM, Ford, or maybe even Volkswagen. I applied and got accepted into two art schools, both of which had very good industrial design departments. One of them was in Detroit, right there in the shadow of GM and Ford. Still to this day, I watch car shows on TV, I subscribe to *Motor Trend* and *Car & Driver* magazines, I collect model cars and license plates, and I am fascinated with the world of car design. I truly love all things automotive. (My love affair with Beetles morphed into one with Mini Coopers over the past 10 years, but that's a whole different story!) My future felt like it was going to be pretty clear, and I knew that I was going to become a car designer. Looking back at that three-year-old me, standing in the front seat of that Volkswagen Beetle in the photograph, I didn't realize at the time how important that moment was to me.

My family has a long history being followers of Jesus, and that's how I was raised. To this day, I am a follower of Christ. I sign off of every podcast by saying, "*Jesus is King.*" I believe that the world would be a better place if those who follow Him actually acknowledge Him within their day-to-day. It's important to show your love for Him and to live by His golden rule, which is to treat people the way that you want to be treated. If the world would actually live by that, it would be a much better place for everyone.

As I grew up, I got involved in youth groups and church camps, which is where my story takes a turn. Church camp is actually the reason why I didn't turn out to be a car designer. I had every intention to do so, but God had other plans for my life. Let me explain. I loved church camp so much as a kid that I wanted to stay for the entire summer, but the only way to do that was to become a counselor. As a junior in high school, I decided that I would apply to become a camp counselor so I could spend my summers at Camp Christian in Burns, Tennessee, just outside of Nashville. Throughout middle school and high school, I was there every single summer as a camper. Between my junior and senior years, I spent my whole summer there.

One night that summer, we had just turned the lights out at bedtime in the dorm, and all of the counselors decided to go outside to the fire ring and hang out. There we were all lying in the grass and looking up at the stars. We were chatting about normal teenager topics, telling jokes, and sharing funny stories. I still remember looking up at the bright stars in the sky above and feeling very fulfilled and content. It was a contentment that I hadn't experienced many times in my life before then, but I just knew at that moment that I felt happy. I started thinking about my future that night and trying to figure out what I really wanted to pursue. I had already been accepted to those art schools by this time, and I thought my future was set. But something in me was changing. What did I really want to do with my life? We were teenagers who had come from all different towns across the southeast. Our lives had collided that special summer at camp. Because of that shared experience, we forged amazing friendships.

Now, this was at a time before social media or cell phones. I'm sad to say that I ended up losing touch with most of those friends over the years. But that night, laying on my back and looking at the stars, the course of my life changed forever. I didn't really know it at the time, but it did. Those friends were part of that story. All summer, I thought about how much fun I was having at camp. I was always happy and so full of joy. I was making a difference in the world through these kids. That same evening, I decided that was what I wanted to do for a living. My passion was to make a real impact on people's lives, and I knew that I wanted to help kids not only come to know Jesus but to also live fulfilled, productive lives. Being a car designer just wasn't going to give me that same feeling of impact. I knew I was making a decision that my heart had led me to make, and I changed the course of my life that very night.

A lot of people would refer to this type of feeling as a "calling" and I certainly wouldn't disagree. Whatever the correct term, I changed my mind and decided to go into youth ministry. I enrolled at Lipscomb University in Nashville, Tennessee, which is a private Christian college. I was accepted into their youth ministry program and even received a few scholarships to help my parents pay for my education. Without my church camp experiences, I would have never found that passion and pursued a career in ministry. I started working in the ministry scene my senior year of high school, after I got back from church camp that summer, and continued for seven more years. After that, I served as the senior pastor of a local church. Altogether, I spent 13 years in pastoral ministry.

The reason I'm telling you this story is because I want you to understand my background and history before I became an entrepreneur. All of these experiences are what led me to write this book. Those first 13 years of my adult career were spent working with teenagers and adults. I assisted in every aspect of the church, helping to build a stronger community for the Kingdom of God. But after those 13 years, I started feeling upset about how things were being handled. I won't get too far into that discussion, but I knew that it was time for me to move on. I wasn't able to make the same impact or difference that I once had, and I was feeling extremely frustrated by that. After some time, I made another decision that would change the course of my life again. It was a difficult decision, but I decided to leave vocational ministry and go back to school at Lipscomb University. This time, I got a Master's in Education and went into the school system as an eighth-grade history teacher.

For the first time in a long time, I began to feel that same sense of fulfillment and joy again within my profession. Being a school teacher was a phenomenal job. I knew that God had created me to be a teacher, and I loved doing it. The kids liked me too, and they were excited to come to class to learn. I got along well with the other teachers and the administration. Next, I decided to further my education and went on to get my license as a school administrator. My plan was to be in education for the rest of my life, but the Great Recession of 2008-2009 began to affect school systems all over the country. My local school district began feeling the effect, and I wasn't yet tenured. In fact, I happened to be the last guy hired in the entire building where I was teaching. Unfortunately, when they had to make budget cuts, I was the first one to go. That was a heartbreaking moment for me, because I really felt like I was supposed to be in the classroom. After all, I was the #1 teacher in my county in my subject matter – but that didn't matter. My life was about to change once again.

I wasn't prepared for or expecting this change. The first time I changed careers, I was the one who decided to do so. Now, I was being forced to leave the world of teaching against my will. I wanted to stay. I wanted to continue teaching. I wanted to be someone who could help the students and mold their lives. I wanted to help the community become a better place by giving back to the kids. However true, I found myself being forced out of that position. Once again, I had to start asking myself: *What should I do now?*

Well friends, that's how I became an accidental entrepreneur. My first choice was actually to go back into teaching somewhere, somehow. I thought that I'd try to get a job in another county or district, but frankly, there were no teaching jobs to be found anywhere. I was back to square one, and I had no idea what I was going to do next.

Right before this time, one of my friends had approached me to ask if I'd like to start a business together. I didn't really have the desire to become an entrepreneur, nor did I have the valid experience that I thought it took to become a business owner. However, he was persuasive and I acquiesced. We started the business a year prior to my contract ending with the school system. Little did I know that the timing couldn't have been more perfect. When we started the business together, I still thought that I was going to be a teacher forever. This was just a side hustle, which I never intended to become my full-time career. When my teaching contract didn't get renewed, I still thought I'd try to go back to school the next fall when things were a little better with the economy. In the meantime, I started asking myself: *How am I going to make money? How am I going to pay the bills? Will I be able to provide for my family?*

I decided that I needed to actually give this business a shot as a full-time gig. Of course, it was going to require significant changes in regards to how it was being run. For example, the business originally started out in the world of hydrogen generators and ethanol, which again was not my specialty. This was something that my friend had an interest in, and I enjoyed assisting him. But out of necessity, I decided I was going to make a change. I needed to step things up and start working full-time in the company. We ended up going into LED lights, which I thought could become a big opportunity… turns out I was right!

For most of my ministry career, I also sold life and health insurance to small business owners as a way to supplement my meager ministry income. I knew how to sell. I was actually very good at sales. Because of that, I felt like I could sell lighting projects to large commercial companies and buildings all over the country. This was how I knew that I could make this business work.

I gave myself a deadline and told my wife that if there was no traction or money coming in by August 15, 2011, I would go get "a real job" somewhere else. The reason I chose that date is because it was the day I'd be getting my last paycheck from the county school system. Three days before that self-imposed deadline, I walked into a local hospital and gave the pitch of a lifetime. If you've ever heard me speak before, you probably recall the story of that sales call. It was epic, and they bought the project from me! It turned out to be a $2.3 million undertaking over the next few years. And because of this, my accidental entrepreneurship became a reality.

Over the next seven years, I built that business up to multimillion-dollar status. Twice, we were listed on *Inc. Magazine's* 5000 list as one of the "Fastest Growing Privately Held Companies in the Country." We were also printed in *Entrepreneur's* 360 list as one of the "Top Entrepreneurial Companies in the Country." The *Nashville Business Journal* recognized us as one of the "Top Small Businesses of the Year," and we also were named "Best in Business." I was personally nominated for Sumner County's Impact Award and the *Nashville Business Journal's* "Top 40 under 40" when I was 39. My company also won "The Rising Star" award from the Tennessee Small Business Development Center. The awards kept coming and we continued to build an amazing business.

Things were going extremely well until I finally realized that this wasn't the lifestyle I wanted to live. I had become an accidental entrepreneur. I started doing this just to make ends meet, and believe me I made much more money than I ever would have as a school teacher or a minister. But the lifestyle I had taken on by accident wasn't making me happy. I was the President and CEO of a multimillion-dollar company, but I wasn't living my life in the way that I wanted to. I was never passionate about LED lighting or electrical contracting-–I got into this world out of pure necessity and opportunity. It's true that so many entrepreneurs do the exact same thing. They find themselves selling products or providing services that they don't actually have any real passion for. They don't have any joy or fulfillment in what they're doing, other than they're paying the bills and making sure the business continues to operate. Others continue running their businesses simply out of duty or obligation. You then have to make sure that things operate well, while being mindful of your employees, and keeping income coming in so that you can take care of your family. The list goes on.

There's no shame at all in doing a job out of necessity, and there's nothing wrong with building up a business simply to earn an income. But what if you could have it all? What if it was possible to have the business *and* the income, but to also build a lifestyle for yourself that allowed you to not be so heavily involved? What if it was possible to live the exit lifestyle and still own the business?

That thought never even occurred to me when I was first starting out. It was never the goal, because I didn't think it would ever be possible to get out of the daily operations of the business. I was acting as the President and CEO–I was the guy that handled everything. I was the number one salesperson, the contact when things went wrong, the leader of each team, and I was doing many of the tasks within the business. I had a great team, but I was acting as the hero and not allowing them to run the business without my input. This kept me trapped, and I didn't realize it at the time.

In late 2017, I hired my first business coach named BJ Howard. We ended up becoming great friends over the course of his mentorship. I even introduced him to another friend of mine, and they later became business partners. Sadly, BJ passed away unexpectedly in 2020. Rest in peace, BJ.

He was the first person who pointed out to me that I was trapped in the ironic prison of entrepreneurship. BJ helped me see that my life was meant for something more than running the day-to-day operations of a lighting and electrical company. It was evident to him that I loved my business and my employees, but I didn't love doing the business day in and day out. He understood my predicament and asked me lots of great questions, as a good business coach should. At some point, I asked him, "*Why don't I sell the business?*" This seemed to me like a natural question to ask in this scenario.

In terms of revenue, we were doing well, though we had some debt that was caused by a national account not paying us on time. But BJ reluctantly shared something with me that changed my perspective. He said:" *Jason, you could try to sell, but your business really isn't worth anything. Of course, your revenue is strong and you are profitable. You've got a great team with a great product, and a great reputation in the industry. You've established the brand, but it's not worth anything. Do you know why? Because whoever buys this company will need you. They would want to buy you, and you therefore wouldn't be released."*

I knew that what he said was completely correct. In order to move on, I had to figure out some other way to do it. Reality hit me right between the eyes, just like it did Edward. The business wasn't really worth as much as I thought it would be, because it required me to be the hub in the center of the wheel. I was the hinge upon which the whole business turned; I was the hero. This unfortunately put me in a position of being the main asset of the company. I was the thing that made the company valuable. Like Edward, the best I could hope for was an earnout, and I didn't want that at all.

I began to think: *"If I can't sell the business for anything on the open market, what are my other options? How do I get out of the daily grind of this business that is not giving me the lifestyle that I want?"* I knew there were other businesses that I would enjoy owning. In fact, I knew that if I could go back and start again, I would have never started a business in this industry. It's not that I regret my decision, but it was a difficult business to be invested in. We rode the wave at the right time, and we succeeded because of that. However, I would never want to go back and do it again in the same industry.

Instead, maybe I'd go into the motorcycle business or the car business – maybe I'd go back to those early childhood aspirations and revisit my love affair with cars. I thought about pursuing that dream for a minute, but there wasn't much of an option for moving into that field without taking large steps backwards in terms of my income. I quickly realized there simply weren't any good options in that world.

Instead, over the next 18 months, I made the decision to dive deep into the concept of delegation so that I could emancipate myself from the ironic prison I had built unintentionally. I didn't know much, but I knew that if I could learn to truly delegate the right way, I'd eventually be able to get out of the weeds of daily operations. I desperately wanted to figure out a way to make myself free, and I didn't want to be required to sit in my office every day. I wanted to have the ability to be away from the office and even work on a new project if I chose to, while also continuing to receive an income from the business that was operating successfully in my absence.

Besides delegation, I learned that stress was a major reason why the business always needed me. If I was ever going to be able to get out of the weeds, I was going to have to learn how to manage and eliminate stress – not just my own but the stress of my employees, as well. In addition to that, I began working on developing systems and processes so that I wouldn't be required to physically be present each day. And finally, I began investing more deeply in my team members and especially my leadership team. These four core principles are what allowed me to ultimately work from anywhere. They gave me the freedom to walk away from the daily operations of that business in January 2020. Of course, that was a time when the whole world was turned upside down by the COVID pandemic, but my commitment to these four core principles (that I will explain in detail later in this book) protected the viability of my company even in the midst of 2020's uncertainty.

For the first few months after stepping away from the daily operations, I checked in with my leadership team once a week. They were managing things well, despite the pandemic. After time passed and everything felt like it was solidly in place, I was able to move on to focus on a new project. But what would that be? Honestly, it took me about 4 to 5 months before I felt like I knew what I was supposed to be doing. The truth is that I went through an identity crisis during those first six months after stepping away from the role as President and CEO. For 10 years, I had carried business cards that told people I was President and CEO of Energy Lighting Services. That's how people knew me. Now that I was no longer running the daily operations – even though I still owned the business – who was I? How would I introduce myself? What was I going to do with the time I now had?

For the past five years, I had been coaching a few entrepreneurs to help them start, grow, and scale their businesses. Because I had experienced success as an entrepreneur, people would often come and ask me for advice, and I was happy to give it. At that point, I wasn't charging for my services, but I really loved the experience. During a lunch with one of my mentors, about four months after I stepped out of the owner-operator role, he suggested I formalize my coaching services and start a coaching company. He told me: *"Jason, people will want to do what you've done – they will want to exit their businesses without necessarily selling them just like you have. You just need to formalize the process, and people will pay you good money to learn it."*

That was it! I loved the idea. It combined all of my gifts and skills as a former pastor, teacher, and entrepreneur. I would be able to make an impact on this world by helping other entrepreneurs get their lives back and escape the ironic prison of entrepreneurship. I would be instrumental in giving wives their husbands back from the companies that steal so much of their time. Kids would finally get their dads back, and they could become more involved in their lives because they would have time to focus on what's most important, rather than what is urgent in the business. It was finally becoming clear to me that this was what I was put on the earth to do.

When I took a moment to actually realize all that I had accomplished and all that my team was now able to do in my absence, I discovered that I had given the business a stable foundation from which to operate. I had exited the business without selling. I was able to walk away successfully from the day-to-day tasks, the stress, the operations, and the pressure of 70+ hour weeks. Now I could be more involved in other passions, while also still getting paid and still receiving the tax benefits of business ownership.

IT'S POSSIBLE FOR YOU, TOO

People wanted to know what I did. Did I sell the company? Was everything ok? I didn't know what to call it at the time, so I just told people that I pulled off an exit without exiting. That phrase stuck and it's now the method I teach thousands of entrepreneurs all over the world. And it is the method I will teach you in this book. The method I coined *exit without exiting* is what will lead you to the exit lifestyle sooner than you ever thought possible.

Exit without exiting allowed me to live the lifestyle that I had wanted for so long as an entrepreneur. I could now work from home, from the road, or from anywhere. I could travel with my wife and my kids. We could go do things that we had always dreamed of doing but never had the time to do. This was the lifestyle that I desired, and it was created by the choices that I made over time.

The lifestyle that you live right now was created because of the choices that you made and the actions you've taken. If it isn't what you want, it is no one's fault but your own. It is the natural result of every decision you've made up to this point in your life. If you are trapped in your business like I was, like Edward was, and like Cheryl was, it's because you have chosen to be the hero. You created this prison. However, it doesn't have to stay this way forever.

Just like your current lifestyle is the result of the decisions you've made up until now, the lifestyle you will live five years from now will be based on the decisions you make today. You can actively pursue choices that lead you towards the exit lifestyle. This way of living opens up your life tremendously, and you've made a great first decision by reading this book. Although true, the magic only happens in the action. Reading this book is not enough – you have to act. You have to put these four core principles into *action* in your life and your business. By taking action, you will change your life forever and begin truly experiencing your version of the exit lifestyle.

Think about what the exit lifestyle will be for you. What is it going to mean for you today? *Will I start another business, will I travel, will I stay home and spend time with my family, will I go work at a soup kitchen, will I do something for my mental or physical health?* The choice is yours, and all of the options are at your disposal when you decide to exit without exiting. That's the beauty of this method. It opens up your options and allows you to live the lifestyle you truly desire. No longer will you not have a choice in what you do each day. No longer will you lack control over your decisions. The exit lifestyle can provide you with an almost limitless amount of options.

Let's think about Cheryl again from Chapter 1. When she received her big, life-changing check, her ability to have choices now defined her new lifestyle. For her husband, it was an Aston Martin. For her, it was a new house. How did Edward's lifestyle change? Maybe it changed a little bit for a short amount of time, but he didn't really have the same full benefits. This is because he was still chained to the office. Then, think about James... he's a lot like me. James built up a successful business, and he was able to see that his lifestyle now had the potential to change. He was given a lot of the same options as Cheryl. Of course, he never had the same checkbook as Cheryl has, but he understands that time is more important than money. It's a renewable resource and something that you can't get back once it's gone. Cheryl traded 10 years of grinding and putting in long hours for a huge payday. In the end, she missed a decade of her kids' lives that she can never recreate. While James maybe couldn't achieve the financial freedom that Cheryl got after her exit, his exit without exiting provided him with tons of time to spend with his family. In the end, Cheryl missed that and regretted it. Personally, I'd rather be like James.

I've said this before, and I'll say it again: money is a renewable resource. It can be replenished after it's spent, but time cannot. If you do it correctly, the exit lifestyle can provide you with both time and money. It's all about getting to live your life on your terms. No, you do not have to sell your business to achieve this lifestyle. You can change your life forever if you make this method your goal. As we've discussed, only 2% of entrepreneurs receive the big check that offers them time and freedom. For the other 98%, it's time to focus on a new goal – one that's more realistic. You can live the exit lifestyle now, and you don't have to wait until later down the road. Unfortunately, that may never even happen. It is possible to design a life that you love right now – one that gives you the time and freedom that you need in order to live your life in the fullest way possible. This book is going to give you all the tips and tricks necessary to achieve this for yourself. Just know this: it's absolutely possible and you can do it. Don't worry! This won't take you nearly as long as you think it will. You can make a huge shift in your life within the next 12 to 18 months. You'll be able to change your lifestyle, the lives of your family members, and your employees if you commit to it.

3. WHY YOU NEED TO LIVE THE EXIT LIFESTYLE

It's time to ask yourself: *What were your goals when you originally started your company? What did you see happening long-term?* When I started my company as an accidental entrepreneur, my goal was to simply pay the bills. That was it – I was in full-on survival mode. I didn't have any type of long-term goals that I wanted to set out to achieve far into the future. I wasn't planning to create some huge organization and become a millionaire. Now granted, that's what happened, but that wasn't my pursuit. I simply wanted to survive.

Most people don't start businesses the same way that I did. Instead, many entrepreneurs have a specific goal to build something much larger than themselves. They purposefully enter into the world of entrepreneurship in order to create something that makes an impact and also helps them to gain a lot of money. This is why entrepreneurs do what they do. At the core, an entrepreneur is someone who takes big risks that other people aren't willing to take. They innovate things in new ways that other people have never even thought of, which in turn makes the world a better place.

That's you! You are an entrepreneur. You are a risk-taker, an innovator, and you are changing the world.

I believe that it's entrepreneurs like you and me who actually have the capacity to *change the world.* Within our day-to-day work, we make a bigger impact on the world than pastors, teachers, or even parents. That's a bold statement, but it's one that I think is completely valid. I was a pastor. I was a teacher. I am now a parent. While I did make an impact in each of these roles, I'm making a bigger impact on the world as an entrepreneur. Why and how do I know that? It's a simple fact that everything you enjoy in life was created by an entrepreneur. It's true! Besides the things that come from nature, such as the beauty of a mountain range, the tranquility of a river running through the woods, the majesty and power of a waterfall, or the complex fragrances of a rose garden, everything else we enjoy in life has been created through the spirit of entrepreneurship.

The cell phones that we use every day. The conveniences of the homes we live in. The shoes we wear when we go for a run. The Internet we use to learn new concepts and stay connected to friends and family. The ways in which we read or listen to books like this one. The medical care we receive when we are sick. Everything we enjoy and benefit from came from the mind of an entrepreneur. These things help to change our world, and entrepreneurs are the force behind that change. That notion of change-making is often why people start businesses. They want to make a real impact and leave a legacy within the world. They want to do things that can make the world a better place.

And that's what you want to do, too.

THE REAL MEANING OF SUCCESS

As you consider the reasons why you started your business to begin with, ask yourself: *Do I have what I hoped for? Have I achieved this? Am I living the life I want to live?* The true definition of success is getting the results that you intended to achieve. Basically, when you first started your company, if you wanted to have more time, more money, and more freedom, and now you've found yourself without those things, you're not succeeding. This is exactly what most people think when they start a business: *I want to be my own boss, I want more time, I want more money, and I want more freedom.*

Ask yourself: *Do I have that? Am I achieving those things? Am I living the lifestyle that I want to live?* What ends up happening most of the time is that you don't actually have more time. You don't even have more freedom, because you become so strapped to your business. Yes, many entrepreneurs end up earning more money than their W2 counterparts; however, they don't have the time or freedom to spend it as they see fit.

I know a multitude of entrepreneurs. When you own a business, you naturally meet other business owners. I have a friend who owns 16 companies, and he's the first person that I have ever met who earns more than a million dollars in annual income. He's far surpassed that mark now, but he has very little time and freedom. He has tons of money, but can't actually enjoy his life because he's become completely trapped by his success. He's stuck in his business and with all of the things that he has to do every single day in order to keep those companies running properly. When looking at the pros and cons, you have to analyze your lifestyle. Are you getting what you want? Have you become your own boss? Are you in charge of how you're living your life? Do you have the choice and control to live your daily life as you desire? Could you decide tomorrow that you want to take a month off?

Or...have you become a prisoner inside of your own company?

LIVING THE EXIT LIFESTYLE

You didn't start your business to have a better job; you started it to have a better life. This is exactly why you must adopt the exit lifestyle – this way, you can have your cake and eat it too. You can own the business but also be free to step away and live life on your own terms. You want choices, and you want control. It's easy to get off balance when you're first starting a business. You think you're working toward attaining what you set out to do when you began, but then you end up getting tied down and disconnected from your life outside of work. In reality, the exit lifestyle is exactly what you wanted – you just weren't aware that it even existed.

I'll let you in on a little secret... *it does exist, and you can have it.*

Only masochists would get up every single morning and say: *It's my lifelong goal to go to my company every day for the rest of my life, just to work hard and be stressed out all the time!* The reality is, that's what the lives of most entrepreneurs look like. They work hard. They're stressed out. They're hanging by a thread from the end of a rope. They're working all the time and really hustling. Is that what you wanted when you set out to change the world? Not me.

The sad reality is that most entrepreneurs who are living that lifestyle – which I like to call the ironic prison of entrepreneurship – are not enjoying the benefits of business ownership. This is actually the very opposite of the exit lifestyle concept. Unfortunately, they continue doing it because they don't see a way out. Most of them, like Cheryl and Edward, are just waiting until a later date to retire or sell the business and walk away. They work day in and day out in order to one day leave and finally get some freedom. However, that "one day later" could be today. Instead, like James, they could adopt the exit lifestyle and not have to wait.

Think about it this way. Why would employees work from the ages of 20 to 65, only to retire and then live for 15 years on a small chunk of what they used to live on while they were working? Why would you put 45 years into something, as an employee, to then live only 15 years in retirement? You don't want to do that; in fact, nobody wants to do that. Entrepreneurs leave the rat race exactly for that reason – so they don't end up having to live that lifestyle.

Yet, ironically that's how most entrepreneurs end up living out their lives. They don't have the 401(k), but they're still living as if they're waiting until some unspecified date in the future when they'll eventually be able to "retire" and get out of the daily grind of running the company.

There's a very successful author named Mike Michalowicz, whom I interviewed on my podcast, *The Root of All Success* in June of 2021 (episode #051). He's written tons of books, has a podcast himself, and is a public speaker and coach. One of the best books of all time on business (in my humble opinion) was written by him called *Profit First.* I got the chance to dive deeper into his story of origin during our chat on my show. His first business was in the tech space, and he built a very successful company from scratch. Later down the road, he sold it for a good sum of money but not that life-changing amount that we've been discussing. He had enough to be very comfortable for a while, but he was going to have to continue working.

I asked him how much money he was paying himself while he was actually running the company before he sold it. He answered: *very little. Not even enough to pay the mortgage! It was less than $20,000 per year.* I then asked him if he could go back and do things differently, would he have paid himself more? He said yes, of course. For him, the meager salary he paid himself just to have a future payday at a sale wasn't worth it. If he would have paid himself what he was worth when the business first started, that same business would have been worth far more in the end.

He went on to start another company, which he built and actually did sell for a life-changing amount of money. But once again, he didn't make any money until he actually sold it. I asked him the same question: *Would you have paid yourself more during the scaling phase if you could do it all over again?* Guess what he said: *yes!* The fact that he didn't pay himself correctly during the scaling of the business actually devalued the company, because the company was not accustomed to paying a CEO a fair wage. The buyers had to factor that into their valuation and offered less money to offset the new CEO salary they'd have to build into the budget. However, he had to get through many years of small paychecks in order to fulfill this dream. That's exactly why he wrote the book, *Profit First.* He wanted to teach new entrepreneurs – just like I try to teach entrepreneurs – how to set themselves up for success by paying themselves first. In his book, he speaks directly to finances and how to manage that part of owning a business. He wants entrepreneurs to be able to take their profit first. The goal when you start a company is to earn money for you – not to pay your employees, not to pay your shareholders, not to pay anyone else. You created this business for yourself, so why take so much time to actually bring home the money? You can have it now. It's time to stop waiting.

Let me ask you a question. What would you do if you were able to exit your company today? What would that look like? What would you do if tomorrow you didn't have to go to work, but you kept getting paid? Let's assume that you've paid yourself the appropriate salary that a CEO of a company your size would make. If you're doing what my friend Mike was doing and you're only paying yourself $20,000, that's the first thing you need to fix. But let's say you're making $500,000 as the CEO of a small, privately held company. The business is making somewhere between $5–$10 million a year in revenue. If tomorrow you didn't have to go into the office, or next month, or for the next year, what would you do with your life? You're still getting your $500,000 a year in income from the business. You still own the business. You still get the tax write-offs and the added benefits of being a business owner. Think about what you would do, knowing that the business was running perfectly fine without you, and you never had to be there. How would you live your life? Where would you go? Where would you choose to live, now that you don't have to be there? Whatever your answer may be, that's your own personalized *EXIT LIFESTYLE.* It's important to understand that you can have that now. It becomes possible, once you begin thinking and moving towards this goal now instead of waiting for some future payday at a big exit.

There's a lesson to learn here that has to do with renewable and non-renewable resources. A renewable resource is something that you can get back after consuming it. A nonrenewable resource is something that you can never get back after it's gone. Think about time as nonrenewable. Once you spend it, you can never have it back. Ever! Money, on the other hand, is a renewable resource. The money you spend today is gone, but you can make more of it tomorrow. What I always like to showcase to my clients in coaching is that time is the most valuable of our resources. You have to consider making investments by leveraging your renewable ones for nonrenewable ones. In other words, if you can spend money to get time, do it! But don't ever spend time to get money. That is not a good investment. Time is more important than money, because you need time to do anything and everything that you want to do with your days. At the end of life, you will not look back and wish for more money, but you will wish you had more time.

If you said: *Jason, I want you to invest $100,000 into this program. In doing so, you will get an entire year added back onto your life. You don't have to do anything, except invest a hundred grand and you get a whole year back. You can do anything you want with the time.*

Well, of course, I'm going to be spending that hundred grand! You don't even have to try to sell that idea to me. I will pay it right now, without any resistance. If you think about it this way, a hundred grand is an exceptional deal for that amount of time. You need to start thinking about time in this capacity, because it's truly your most valuable asset. It's a commodity that never comes back to you once it's been spent. This idea of waiting until much later into the future, telling yourself that one day you'll be able to sell and live your life on your own terms is not the way to do things. You're simply spending so much time that you'll never have again.

Cheryl sold her business for more money than she'd ever be able to spend in a lifetime, but at the closing table, she realized how much time she had missed with her kids in their teenage years. Years that she could never get back. Was it all worth it?

Edward worked long hours and missed lots of time with his wife and kids in hopes that he'd be able to sell his business one day and have financial freedom. It didn't materialize for him, and he regretted the lost time.

James was able to capitalize on both time and money. He designed his business to pay him a passive income that would allow him all the time he wanted to spend with his family and even time to go start a new business. He leveraged a bit of his personal income to get time. That was a great investment.

I'm now 47 years old. I was 35 when I started my first company. If I could go back now and start that company, or if I could have started my life as an entrepreneur in my twenties – knowing what I know now – I would be a billionaire. I would have all the time in the world, and all the money in the world, to do whatever I wanted to do. Unfortunately, though, I got started too late and I didn't learn the value of time until I was in my mid-forties. Time doesn't slow down; it keeps moving forward, whether you're ready or not. If you're in your twenties or thirties, get started today! Every day that you wait is just another day that you won't get back. Every dollar that you spend is a dollar that you can get back. Spend money on a coach, a mastermind, or a mentor who will help you leverage your business and financial resources so you can live the exit lifestyle today. If you have an opportunity to go to a conference or enroll in a program to learn how to do this, do it! These things will help you to see that in order to get your time back, you have to spend the money first. The exit lifestyle is all about attaining the time to do what you want, because it's more important than money. Spend the money now, in order to get time back later.

Let me tell you a personal story about how I live the exit lifestyle. In 2018, we made a decision to purchase what we thought was our dream home on a road called Upper Station Camp Creek Road in Sumner County, Tennessee, just north of Nashville. For all of my adult life, I've ridden motorcycles down Upper Station Camp Creek Road, because it is one of the best riding roads in the area. There was this one house I always remembered that sat way back off the road. It was a beautiful 5,000-square-foot home on seven and a half acres. There was a gorgeous plot of land with a barn, a paved driveway, a gate, and a picturesque view. I remember riding by all of those years thinking: *Wow, I'd love to live in a house like that, but I'll never be able to afford it.* At the time, I was in ministry and working as a school teacher. We definitely couldn't afford a large home of that capacity. But in 2018, we were in a much different financial position and decided to buy the house next door to the one I'd always admired, which I had never noticed because it was hidden by trees. After we moved in and began getting familiar with the new house and the land, we befriended our neighbors and I shared this story with them. *"Well, congratulations on getting the home of your dreams,"* they said. I was confused. While we absolutely loved our new place, it wasn't their house. It wasn't the one I had dreamed of all those years as I rode by on my motorcycle. *"Our houses are exactly the same,"* the husband said. *"The people who built these homes were good friends and used the same plans to build their homes next to one another."* I was blown away. We ended up getting the house of our dreams by accident.

We made so many memories in that home. When we moved in, I was still President and CEO of Energy Lighting Services and was running that company full-time with no other duties. In 2019, I began to create my own exit plan, and in January 2020, I exited the daily operations of that company. By the end of 2020, I was 100% out of the daily operations. For the entire year of 2021, I had zero duties and nothing to do with the company other than owning it. I signed papers and made sure everything was taken care of from a financial and legal perspective, but otherwise, I had no major responsibilities. I brought in a new CEO to run the daily operations. I set him up with an excellent leadership team and wonderful employees who were killing it. They were doing such a fantastic job, in spite of everything that was going on in the world during that time.

When I exited my company, my lifestyle began to change drastically. My coaching business started to take off, and since it didn't require me to be in any one location at any certain time, we started going on trips in our RV for about a week every month. Today, we are essentially gone for at least a quarter out of every year. On our last big trip of 2021, we took a two-week trip down to Key West. While we were on that trip, my wife and I began having deep, contemplative conversations about our lifestyle and what we wanted for the future. Our son had moved out and our daughter was 19 at the time, fully involved with her church, friends, and two jobs. We figured that over the next few years, she would also be moving out to start her life on her own. Soon, it would be just the two of us. We love to travel, and we knew that we wouldn't have anyone to take care of this large home and the land when we were away. There's so much to take care of: the pool, the pond, the gate, the fences, the barn. Once again, our lifestyle was changing, and this home didn't really fit in anymore. What we really wanted more than anything was to be free, to travel, and be on the road. We wanted to see new areas of the country that we hadn't seen before and go hit the road in our RV.

At the end of 2021, on our trip to Key West, we made the decision to sell the house. It was such a tough call, but it was no longer our dream home. We had other aspirations. Much to our surprise and delight, the house had gone up 74% in value since we bought it. We had suspected that it had gone up in value, but not that much. When we finally made the decision to put it on the market, we received over-asking price offers before it was even listed. Ultimately, it sold it for more than we imagined we would get for it… it was almost like winning a small lottery.

Now that we've sold it, we're completely free to live however we want to live. We made this choice because we know that we can't get time back. Right now, we are renting a house just down the street that is half the size and has only 5% of the upkeep of the old house. We wanted to stay local and continue to have a presence in the community, but we're now free to travel and be wherever we want to be. We decided to take all the money that we were spending on a mortgage and the profits from selling the house and roll that cash into real estate that will make us money – something that will provide us income – so that our exit lifestyle can continue to grow. In September of 2022, we purchased our first short-term rental, which is a cabin in The Great Smoky Mountains of Tennessee. Now that we are using our money to get a return rather than just a place to live, our ability to make an impact for our family and friends can also flourish.

The house is just another example of how I make my lifestyle decisions. At the time we purchased it, the house fit our lifestyle perfectly. But now, it doesn't make sense. Now, it's time to do something different. This is exactly what the exit lifestyle is all about.

Why exactly do you need to live the exit lifestyle? If you want to have freedom to pursue life in the way that you choose, you've got to adopt this mindset. The probability of that happening in your future is based on decisions that you're making today. If you put forth the effort and work with the right people to ensure your success, you can start living the exit lifestyle much sooner than you ever thought possible.

4. REVERSE ENGINEER YOUR EXIT

Now that you understand what the exit lifestyle is and you know that it's possible for you to get there, let's dive into the process a bit deeper. If you want to work toward achieving this, it's time to get serious about your goals. As I explained to you in the last chapter, your overall goals in regards to your business and your lifestyle are going to change dramatically over time. Goals grow. Goals change. Once you hit a goal as an entrepreneur, you will inevitably set a new one. Your desires change, too, over time.

Personally, my goal was to have my dream house. I wanted a big house where I could entertain and have fun with my friends and family. Looking back on that, I can see that my goals evolved slowly over time and have become very different. Today, I want to own rental homes that provide an income and allow me to be able to travel wherever I feel like going. I want to spend my active hours leading my mastermind and coaching entrepreneurs on how to live the exit lifestyle, which I can do from anywhere with an Internet connection. I want to travel with my wife in our RV. I want to take epic cross-country trips on my motorcycle with friends. I'm designing my life around these goals. Being stuck running a business every day, having to go into an office, managing people, negotiating with vendors, and talking to customers is not my idea of the exit lifestyle.

It's important for you to understand that your goals and desires will change as time moves forward. Maybe right now you don't know what those new goals will be, or even the direction that you're going to move in. Just know that it's time to dream big. If you design your business to provide you with the freedom to choose what you do each day, and in a way that you can maintain control over those choices, you are well on your way to living the exit lifestyle without having to wait for some big sale in the future.

YOUR ULTIMATE GOAL

I want to help you reverse engineer your exit. To do so, it's time to begin thinking about what your overall, future, and ultimate goals could potentially be. You'll have to dig a little deeper and look at the future version of yourself to see what it is that you want to go after. I'd like for you to picture where you see yourself far down the road. What is your version of the exit lifestyle? When the author of a book says get out a piece of paper and write something down, almost nobody does it. But I want you to remember that the magic is in the action. All the good stuff happens when you act, not when you read. So go ahead and do this for yourself.

ACTION STEP: Get out a piece of paper and begin visualizing your exit lifestyle. When you write something down, it helps the brain to actualize that thought, and then you're more likely to move forward with the next steps that will make it happen. As I write this, I'm currently doing it for myself in front of a four-foot-tall, eight-foot-long whiteboard. I'm drawing a square in the upper left-hand corner that's about one foot by one foot. Do this with me as an exercise on visualization. Of course, you may be writing on a piece of paper rather than a whiteboard. Just make your square fit on whatever surface you have. (See image 1.1) In that square, write down and clarify your current lifestyle: where you live, what you own, what you drive, the types of clothes that you wear, the impact that you're making in the community, the time that you get to spend with your family, what you're able to do with your time, where you're able to go, and how much money you can give away. Write that in the box, along with anything else that defines your life as it is today. Label that box "TODAY."

Image 1.1

ACTUALIZING YOUR GOALS

On your piece of paper in the very bottom right-hand corner, draw another square of the same size. Look back at that first box on the top left-hand side and survey what's there. Now, in the bottom square start writing down what your ultimate career and lifestyle goals are. What will your version of the exit lifestyle be? I want you to dream really big. Don't hold anything back! Maybe you want to own a Lamborghini or a Ferrari. Maybe you want to have four homes across the country. Maybe you want to move to Spain for part of the year. Maybe you want a house in the south of France, and you want to live there for a quarter of the year. Maybe you want to give away 50% of your income. Maybe you want to be on the board at a local volunteer agency. Maybe you want to host a nonprofit event at your home annually. Perhaps you want to never miss another activity your kids are involved in. Maybe your personal income goal is $3 million annually. These are all noteworthy goals that you can achieve. Whatever you want for your life, write those things in the box at the bottom right hand corner of your paper. (See image 1.2) Label that box "FUTURE."

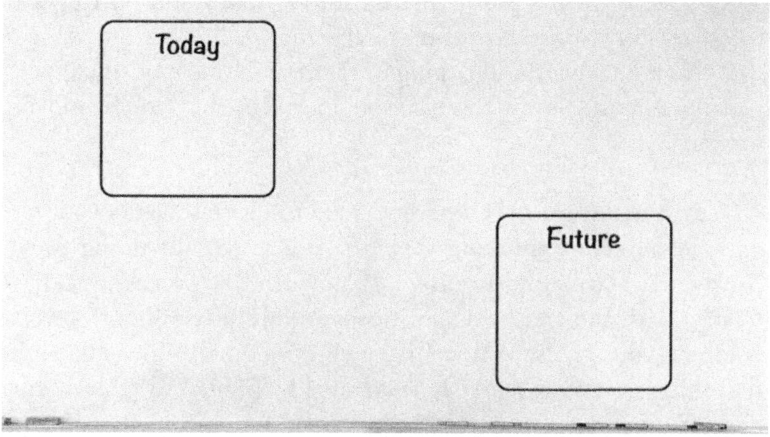

Image 1.2

What most people do – and the concept that most coaches help their clients with – is to work from the top left to the bottom right. Unfortunately, that's wrong. You have to start with the end in mind. Where do you want to go ultimately? What do you want? Start there, and you will be a million times more likely to actually reach your goals. It's the job of a coach to help their client understand how to visualize and go after their goals. Look at the piece of paper in front of you and realize that the box labeled "TODAY" represents what you have and what your lifestyle looks like now. Then, read over what you wrote down in the box labeled "FUTURE," which represents the exit lifestyle that you truly desire. Now, let's figure out how we're going to get everything in that bottom right box to become a reality.

REVERSE ENGINEER YOUR VERSION OF THE EXIT LIFESTYLE

Normally, people go after these goals in the wrong direction. They start from the point where they are today and try to get to the place they want to end up in the future. I'm here to tell you that this is backwards. Working in that way is the opposite of what you need to do, even though you may feel that you're moving forward.

Yes, you always start where you are to move towards your end goal; however, by thinking forwards you're actually doing things backwards. It's counterintuitive, I know. In this process, you have to start with the end goal specifically in mind. It's time to reverse engineer your goals. When I have clients come to me, this is the first thing that we discuss. This is how I help them to achieve their biggest dreams, both within their career and within their overall lifestyle. In order to do so, you have to change the process and start thinking and working differently.

Let's look back at the box diagrams. In the one that's labeled "FUTURE," let's say you've written down that you'd like to own four homes, drive a Ferrari, give away 50% of your income, and earn $3 million annually. To create circumstances to work from, we'll say that right now you're making $500,000, you own one home, you drive a Mercedes, and you give away 10% of your income to charity. In terms of what you have today versus what you want in the future, you feel very far away from attaining your overall goals. The distance between what you have and what you want is vast. You have to change up the process in order to go after what you want.

You need to look at your "FUTURE" box and reverse engineer your way into the exit lifestyle. Before you can own four homes, drive a Ferrari, give away 50% of your income, and make $3 million a year, you will first need to drive a less expensive luxury car, own only three homes, make $2 million dollars a year, and give away 25% of your income. This middle step has to happen before the final step can actually occur. Draw a box just to the left of your "FUTURE" box and write down some things that will be a reality for you *before* you make it to the complete "FUTURE" you're aiming to have. (See image 1.3)

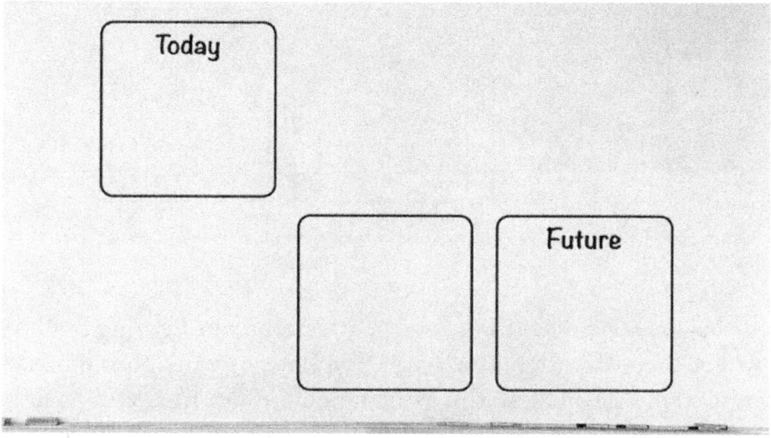

Image 1.3

Then, you need to back up even one more step from there. Draw another box to the left of the last one you drew. (See image 1.4) You need to get to the point where you're making $1 million a year, driving a different luxury car, have one home that you live in and another home that you rent out, etc. This is the process that you have to go through in order to actualize what you really want. There are stepping stones to achieving that final goal, and it's important to be able to move up a step, and then another and another until you reach the final lifestyle that you're hoping to achieve. You keep going through the steps of that process until the box that's in front of you, is the step that immediately comes after where you are today.

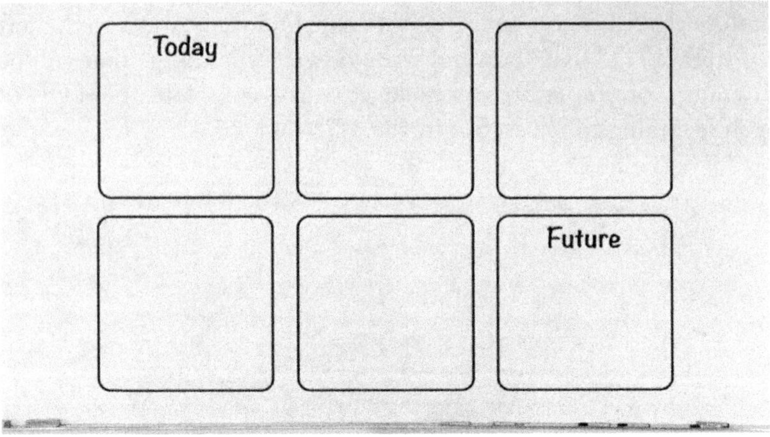

Image 1.4

You're starting with the end goal in mind but figuring out how to get there one step at a time. You have to work through each next step. All of these things come before the final end goal, so you're working to achieve that next step and all that's situated in between the start and the finish line. This is necessary in order to go after and achieve what you *actually* want. Everyone who does this exercise has a different number of steps between TODAY and the FUTURE. Some will have a few and others will have dozens. It just depends on how wide the chasm is between your TODAY and your FUTURE. The point of this exercise is to show you how easy it is to bridge the gap, if you focus on one step at a time rather than the chasm itself.

NAVIGATING YOUR GOALS

Think about a GPS system in a car, or the one on your phone. When you punch in a destination, the software takes your current location – exactly where you are right now – and then creates the easiest pathway to get you where you want to go. When you ask for directions and tell the device what two points you're moving in between, the software isn't thinking: *We have to pull out of his driveway, then let's turn left, and then we get to the end of that street.*

Okay, now we'll turn right, and then maybe we'll turn left.

No, that's not how it works. The GPS looks at the entire route and makes the very best plan of action for getting you from Point A to Point B by routing you in reverse from the destination to your point of origin. In this process, your GPS begins at the very end of the route and starts from there to find the quickest way for you to move forward. This is exactly how the concept of reverse engineering your goals works.

And yes! Sometimes there's construction, or a roadblock, or a big bump in the road. Often, there's an unexplained slowdown and traffic mounts up, causing you to lose time on your route. Assuming Waze or Google Maps knows that – and frequently, they do know these things – they can redirect you around those obstacles. They can route you down another street in order to not get into too much traffic. They can tell you to drive a different way to stay out of a road that's been blocked off for construction. They can design a path for you that's based on the quickest option for getting you to the endpoint destination. This technology will even recalculate your route if you take a wrong turn. That's the concept of reverse engineering your goals, or essentially working you through each step of your trip.

In order to reach your end goals in life, you need to design your exit this exact same way. By doing this exercise, you will route yourself to the exit lifestyle in the quickest way possible. Ask yourself: *Where do you want to be? What's your ultimate goal? How are you going to get there?* Now, let's backtrack those goals to exactly where you are today. This is your Step One.

CASE STUDY

I had a very successful client come to me, who I helped to reverse engineer his goals. We met at my office and went through this exact exercise on my white board together. He, like everyone else, thought that what I was doing was a little bit crazy at first.

He said: *Shouldn't we just start where we are? Isn't that step one? And then, step two, and step three? Eventually, we'll figure out where we want to go.* I told him: *No! We want to discover the end goal first. That's the most important step in the process.*

Once we started writing and filled in that last box with all the details of what he wanted to accomplish, I began asking him more questions. *Before this goal is achieved, what would have to happen?* He answered the questions realistically and thoughtfully. I could feel his wheels spinning within his own mind as we kept moving through the process and the steps. He said: *Ok, before I can own those three houses that I want to own, I'm going to have to make a certain amount of money to get there. I hadn't really thought about that before, which maybe sounds odd. In order to qualify for those mortgages, I'm going to have to make X number of dollars. So I will need to make that amount of money before I can buy those three houses. Before I can make that, I actually have to do this, so that goes in the box before that and the box before that.*

He was getting it. In that moment, he began to see more clearly how he could reverse engineer his own life. When we were finished with the exercise, he realized that the path to what he wanted to achieve was not only possible, but it was also very probable. Most people talk about what's possible in their lives. *Oh, that's possible, I could do that. Yeah, it's possible that I could own four houses. That'd be great. It's possible.* Yes, it is possible to do anything. But is it actually probable? It's never going to be probable if you don't change what you're doing today. The probability of going from TODAY all the way to FUTURE is very low. But the probability of going from the box right before FUTURE into the FUTURE is very high. It's practically guaranteed!

I've always loved the saying: *Nothing changes until something changes.* If you want to own four houses and buy short-term rentals all over the continent, what will you need to do to get there?

It's possible, but is it probable? Every circumstance is only probable if you start making changes to reverse engineer your life.

You have to put yourself in the driver's seat.

Before we wrap up this chapter, I want to remind you again that the magic is in the action. Make sure you take time to reverse engineer your goals. Don't skip this step. You can exit without exiting and start to live the exit lifestyle sooner than you thought possible, but not if you don't take action. If this is an exercise you would like help with, I would be happy to offer my services. You can reach me through my website at:
therealjasonduncan.com/coaching.

5. ACCELERATE YOUR EXIT

In this chapter, I'm going to introduce you to the four core principles that you will need to put in place in order to begin your journey toward the exit lifestyle. First, let's take a minute and revisit my personal exit story before I share my four core principles for learning how to accelerate your exit lifestyle plan.

In 2017, I hired a business coach for the first time and quickly realized that I had trapped myself within the confines of my own company. Yes, I had become very successful. But with the help of my coach, BJ, I started realizing that I was stuck because of the success of my own business. We'd won many awards, we were profitable, and were experiencing growth year after year. Although things were going really well and the company was thriving, I felt consumed and stuck within the success of it all.

When I began thinking about it, I started to understand that I only enjoyed being the CEO of a startup. At this point, my business wasn't a startup anymore. It had grown and reached new heights, and I was no longer in love with the industry that I was working within. The products and services that we were offering weren't even things that I cared that much about. I didn't have any emotional connection or passion for what I was doing on a daily basis. To me, passion is a key indicator of success. At the end of the day, passion is all about your willingness to suffer or endure something difficult for a worthy cause.

PASSION: THE DRIVER OF SUCCESS

By definition, the word *passion* actually means "to suffer." Most people think it's defined as excitement, joy, and happiness. In modern times, that is what most assume when they hear the word passion, but it's so much more than that. And that's not even what the word originally meant. As an example, we refer to the last week that Jesus was on Earth before he was crucified as the "passion of the Christ." We don't call it that because He was excited to be crucified; we call it "passion" because He was willing to suffer for a bigger cause – he was willing to endure for the betterment of others.

I've realized that one of the greatest keys to my own long-term success has been my willingness to endure for things I believe in, which is a character trait that I've always had ingrained in me. In the early years of my accidental entrepreneurship, I had to withstand the difficulties of creating a startup. During those foundational years, there were many business moments or times in the company when things weren't working well. I didn't understand the structure myself, much less how to fix things when they weren't properly running. After all, I was an accidental entrepreneur, and I was trying to figure things out along the way.

My own passion for starting a new business and my willingness to endure is exactly what pushed me through that period of time. I knew that there was a bigger reason behind the business than just me becoming "successful" or making a lot of money. I continued on and even suffered so that my family would have the necessities of life and so that my employees would be able to provide for their families, too. I came out on the other side, and I succeeded all because of my passion and willingness to continue to strive for more, even when times were difficult. However, after my start-up grew into something much greater, I began losing passion. I always tell my clients that seeing the passion for what you're doing dissipate is a sure sign that it's time to get out. This is what motivates us–it's what will contribute to your own success, whatever it is that you're doing. When you find a new business idea that you feel willing to go through difficulties for, that's when you know you're on the right track. It has to be both mentally and emotionally stimulating. That's when the odds of success are even greater.

At the time when I decided to exit the business, my emotional and mental passion for what I was doing was simply nonexistent. I remember having a very personal conversation with my business coach at the time, which helped me through that difficult period of indecision and frustration. We met for lunch and started talking about business in general, and he said: *Jason, if you didn't have this business, what would you be doing? What would you actually want to do?* I remember telling him that I'd love to take all of my knowledge and experiences – everything I knew and had learned along the way about entrepreneurship and business ownership – and build teams to create something new. I told him that ideally, I'd love to own a car or motorcycle dealership, simply because the motorsports industry was something that I had always loved. Instead of building up systems and business structures for a lighting business, I'd be very passionate about working my expertise into a company focused on cars or motorcycles. At least that is what I thought.

But that is not the type of passion that drives success. I love motorcycles and I love cars. It would be fun to own a motorcycle dealership, or to somehow be involved in the car business. As a matter of fact, I attempted to buy two different motorcycle dealerships over the past year, neither of which materialized. I was disappointed at first, but I then realized it would have likely been a big mistake. Why? Because emotional passion (or just liking something) isn't a predictor or guarantee that you'll be successful. After interviewing hundreds of well-versed entrepreneurs on my podcast, *The Root of All Success,* I can confirm that emotional passion doesn't guarantee success. What I found out is that true passion–the kind that allows you to endure and suffer for something greater – is the key to success.

The bottom line is that in order to succeed in anything, you must be willing to go through difficulties. You must have the capacity to get through hardship at times and continue onward. It takes real, true, authentic passion. Just like in a marriage, the relationship will only be as strong as the connection (and passion!) that the husband and wife have. The marriage cannot continue and grow without these things. If there's no passion, and no motivation to get through all of the things that life throws at them, then the marriage will end in divorce. Alternatively, if both spouses have that connection, passion, and willingness to stick it out through sickness and health, for better or worse – that marriage will last. The same is true in business. You will succeed if you have it, but when passion becomes non-existent, the likelihood of success fades quickly.

As promised at the beginning of this chapter, I'm going to share my four core principles with you. These are methods that you can implement into your own strategy while working to exit without exiting and living the exit lifestyle. Remember that they won't work unless you are passionate about making it work. If you, like me, sense that your motivation for the business starts waning, then throw yourself into the pursuit of the exit lifestyle. Your inner drive to get you to the exit lifestyle sooner rather than later will accelerate your path.

These four core principles are your guidelines for finding that ideal life. Think of these methods as ways to gain *choice* and *control.* My principles will solidify your path and start you out on the journey toward the future you truly desire. I'm giving you the keys to unlock your next big adventure as an entrepreneur. By implementing these principles, I was able to step away from the daily operations of a successful company and move on to start several other companies. I put in the work and tested these principles to find out that they work. This is the book I wish my business coach would have shared with me back in 2017 when I was growing tired of running the daily operations of my own company. This is the book I wish I had when I first started my company back in 2010. I'd be much further along my own path and would have avoided a lot of bumps, bruises, and heartache along the way.

I'm going to share all of the main ideas, tips, tricks, and laws that I learned over the past few years so that you will be prepared to begin living the exit lifestyle much quicker than I was able to. This book contains a lot of the coaching information that I offer in my online program called *The 10-Hour Entrepreneur (ExitWithoutExiting.com)*, which is essentially a business accelerator that shows you exactly how to speed up your process according to your ideal timeline. My goal in the course and in this book is to help you push through and speed up your opportunities, choices, and timeline to get you more freedom quicker. Remember, time is the most important resource we will ever have.

There are four core principles that will allow you to exit without exiting, which I am going to share with you. First, let's finish my personal story. During that 18 months, as I tried to figure out how to exit without exiting, I recognized that I had a business structure and partnership that was preventing my business from achieving its maximum potential. I also realized that I had not implemented the right systems early on. While I had amazing employees, I had not invested in my people the correct way, and I had not learned to delegate work and operations correctly. Because of this, I was dealing with a lot of stress, which was in turn affecting my employees and the business itself. When I discovered this and understood what was actually happening, I set out to understand the ways in which I could correct these problems. A year and a half later, I did it. At the end of 2019, I was finally positioned in a place where I could successfully make my exit from the daily operations of the business.

Granted, I do understand that you may not be interested exiting like I did. You may wish to stay involved in the business, but wish you had more time to build assets like James did. You might want to experience a total exit like Cheryl did. I personally was ready to exit, but I still wanted to own the business. As a matter of fact, I still own it to this day as I'm writing this book. However, I was ready to move forward and do something different. I wanted to maintain the business, my employees, the relationships, and the advantages of that business. However, I was also very ready for something different. I knew that I wanted to do public speaking, coaching, and open other businesses – all of which I have now done.

Regardless of what your goals are, these four core principles will help you speed up your ability to do whatever you want to do. With these principles, you will accelerate your path to the exit lifestyle no matter what version of it you want to live. What you and I both know, though, is that you do not want to simply run your business every single day until you can't do it any longer. And if we're being honest, it's not likely that a VC firm is going to waltz in and write you a huge check someday either. Think about it this way: at some point, you will not be involved in your business either by choice or by force. How's the business going to survive without you? To put it even more bluntly, think about this. If you were unexpectedly hospitalized for 30 days and had no contact with your team at the office, what would happen to your business? Would it continue running perfectly every day? Would it close until you return? Would it maintain current customers but struggle to find new ones? If it wouldn't keep running as if nothing changed, you need to implement these four core principles I'm going to reveal over the next four chapters.

CREATING A FASTER EXIT PLAN

I interviewed a gentleman named Dr. Sascha Becker on my podcast (episode #074) in the spring of 2022. He was not my typical guest, because he is not an entrepreneur. When I invited him to be on the show, he first politely turned me down because he was a professor and researcher, not an entrepreneur. I explained to him that his 15-year study on the effects of businesses after the founder dies (Becker, S. (2021). The effects of entrepreneur death on startup performance. Available at: *https://wrap.warwick.ac.uk/147132/13/WRAP-entrepreneur-death-startup-performance-Becker-2021.pdf*) was extremely fascinating and would be of great interest to my listeners. He finally obliged and came on my show.

While we chatted, he spoke about the idea of why you need to accelerate your exit in order to get to a place where your business is not totally reliant on you. He discovered something really interesting through his research: when the founder of a company dies – whether it was expected or not – there was a 60% permanent reduction in revenue. Not only that, the study revealed that there was a 36% permanent reduction in profitability. That is not an insignificant number.

Dr. Becker used the analogy of a business being like a baby. The more you as the parent hold and carry your baby on your own, the less likely the baby is to learn how to feed itself, walk, or grow up naturally and become independent of you. Does that sound familiar? Most entrepreneurs never let their "baby" grow up. We coddle it. We feed it. We carry it on our shoulders. The worst part of this is that we feel like we're doing the right thing.

The study also looked at how devastating the loss of the founder is to most companies. After his or her death, many businesses closed their doors, most struggled, a few maintained their revenue, and only a small handful thrived. The businesses that maintained and thrived were the ones whose founders prepared the company for their absence. They implemented strategies and principles that allowed the business to operate without relying on the influence and daily presence of the founder.

The reality is that you're going to exit your business one way or the other, either voluntarily or involuntarily. With that in mind, you need to prepare your business for your eventual departure. That doesn't have to mean that you give up ownership. That means you get everything in line for you to be able to leave, whether or not you ever actually sell the company. For me, I wanted to exit without exiting so I could explore new projects, new concepts, and new adventures. For you, it may be the need to have more time to build out a new division of your company that you simply don't have time to do now because you're stuck in the weeds every day. No matter which "exit" you wish to achieve, it's all possible. Whatever your personal goal is, the strategy remains the same.

To this day, if something unexpected happens – if I'm struck by lightning, hit by a truck, or have a heart attack – it would not affect my business from an earning or operations perspective. I have set the business up using my four core principles, which can significantly help you to achieve the same stability within your own company. You can also make your business work without you; you simply have to figure out the details and put systems in place so that your presence or absence has very little effect on the actual bottom line of the company.

This way, your revenue still comes in. Your profit still comes in. Your vendor relationships still remain strong. All of the ins and outs of the operational side still happen if you use these four core principles.

I want to give you a brief introduction of what each principle involves, and then I'm going to spend the next four chapters diving deeply into each of these strategies. If you find that you're interested in going through my online coaching program that covers these four core principles, you can sign up on my website at *ExitWithoutExiting.com*. In the course, you'll learn directly from me what each of these principles mean and how to begin implementing them in your own business. Within the course materials, I will take the content that you're about to learn in these next four chapters and unfold it before your very eyes. You'll have homework assignments and projects to work on so that you can accomplish this much and more in an even quicker timeline than when trying to work it out all on your own.

FOUR CORE PRINCIPLES

The first core principle is **Embrace Delegation**. There are so many misconceptions that we have about delegation, but it's going to become the key to making sure that you have trained your employees in the right way to handle tasks that you used to do on your own. When you do this, they're able to perform even in your absence, and in a way that doesn't require you to be looking over their shoulders all the time. You have to embrace it with open arms and learn how to properly delegate work to others.

The second core principle is to **Eliminate Stress**. Stress comes in all shapes, sizes, and forms. There's good stress that can push you harder, and there's bad stress that puts up a wall. You must eliminate all of the bad stress. You'll hear more on this in Chapter 7, but stress is not caused by the endurance of difficult situations. Instead, it's caused by having too many open cycles at any given time. Just like you, most entrepreneurs and business owners run around like a chicken with their heads cut off. In this scenario, you don't have strategies to deal with tasks. You don't know how to handle new tasks when they appear, and you don't know which battles to choose and which to defer. You end up dealing with only what is urgent and not what is most important. What I have learned is that when I was able to eliminate the stress from my life as an entrepreneur, this relief filtered down to my employees. They could see that I was living a more laid back, easier lifestyle. Once they saw me as their leader and a person who was living a stress-free life, they started to embrace the same strategies of eliminating stress for themselves. Once their stress levels went down, the company started operating like a well-oiled machine.

The third core principle is to **Establish Systems and Processes**. Of course, there are dozens of systems and processes throughout every different industry and each type of business. It is not my intent with this book, nor my intent in my coaching program, to help you establish every single system and process that you will need to put in place. I could only accomplish that through a one-on-one coaching program that's specialized and tailored to fit your needs. However, the idea of establishing systems and processes is about making sure that things are being done in your business in a way that's based around a system and a process – not just a personality, not just your own personal whim, not just your desire or your gut instinct on how to get this done. In Chapter 8, I will share the concept with you that the most important system you need to put into place is your sales system. As the number one salesperson in my company for seven years, I began systematizing what I was doing so that my other team members in the sales department could replicate that. This gave me the ability to have predictable revenue as I stepped away from daily operations.

The fourth core principle is to **Invest in People**. This is what we will discuss further in Chapter 9, where we'll dive into what the word invest actually means. We'll also look into how we can leverage people to accomplish our dreams, while giving them exactly what they want as well. You can do this without using or manipulating them. You can invest in them and create a method where there's a return, not only for you as the owner and the founder of the company, but also for them. You want to set things up so that they can also benefit from this new method of doing things. Another thing I'll talk more about is how to find, hire, and onboard people that will help you keep your business running long-term. One of the best things I can say about my business is that I have millennials who work for me that have been with me for nearly 10 years now. That's an amazing feat in today's world, considering that millennials have a reputation for not staying anywhere more than two or three years at a time. Of course, they can quit at any time, but because of the culture that I've built there and the investments that I've made into them both financially and personally, they have stayed. It's so important to maintain a caring, kind, excellent culture inside the business to keep your best employees. I'm going to show you exactly how to implement this core principle in a way that will change your business as a whole.

Let's dive into each core principle and exactly how you can start this process today.

6. EMBRACE DELEGATION

Delegation is not a sexy topic. It's not something that people sign up to take courses on or even learn how to do. The funny thing is that everyone who is a leader must delegate in order to be an effective leader. Why? Because leaders who don't delegate are simply one-man shows who aren't really leading anything. This chapter will guide you through delegation and why it is so important. This is the first of four core principles to accelerate your path to an exit without exiting.

Before we dive in, let's revisit Edward, Cheryl, and James from earlier in the book.

Edward was a terrible delegator. As a matter of fact, it was the one thing he hated doing more than anything else. To Edward, the process of delegating and having to teach someone to do something was a waste of time. After all, no one could do the task better than him, so why give it to someone else who would not do it as well as he would? As you're going to see, the time he "saved" by doing the task himself and not delegating ended up costing him hundreds of thousands of dollars and an extra three years of his life when it came time to exit his business. Because he had not embraced delegation and rather maintained the responsibility for every task, his business was worth much less and the buyer ultimately required him to stick around for three more years to make sure other people could do the tasks that Edward had been doing for years. This is what happens when you do not embrace delegation.

As opposed to Edward, Cheryl was decent at delegating. While she was happy to delegate low level tasks and didn't get involved in most minimum wage activities, she still held onto what she considered the "most important" tasks in the business. Unfortunately for Cheryl, she was under the impression that the most important tasks revolved around client acquisition, product development, and customer service. In reality, the most important tasks for every entrepreneur boil down to three things: setting the vision, communicating the vision, and building the asset. Everything else should be handled by other employees or team members. The problem with Cheryl holding on to those other so-called most important tasks, was that they required lots of time and attention. Time that she ended up stealing from her family. She built a great asset, but unfortunately got caught up in the lie that so many entrepreneurs believe: you must grind and hustle if you want to be successful. If she had been more like James and delegated every task – except the three most important ones I listed above – she would not have missed her kids' most formative years while the business was growing.

James was a master delegator. He embraced it. To James, delegation was the first and most important principle of growing and sustaining a business that would provide him the lifestyle he truly wanted to live. He understood that his business was a tool to provide him the financial resources to live the life he truly wanted. As you're about to see, James embraced delegation in a way that allowed him to build an amazing asset that would give him passive income for many years to come.

THE HERO SYNDROME

Delegation was the first principle that I had to learn in order to exit without exiting. It was this skill – in the heat of the battle of running a company – that actually helped me extricate myself from the ironic prison of entrepreneurship. One that I had to be present for every single day. When I started my company, I was the best at everything I did. I was the best salesperson, the best administrative person, the best finance person, and the best operations person. Every entrepreneur who's started something new could easily say the same thing. When you start your own company, you are the best at everything that your company does. However, that's simply not sustainable for the long run. Eventually, you have to quit being the hero.

There's this thing I refer to as "hero syndrome" which happens when you as the entrepreneur put your cape on, inscribe an S for *Superhero* on your chest, and show up to solve every problem every single day. Every time there's a fire, you're the one who is there to put it out. If your baby is in peril, you show up and save the baby. Everything that goes on within the business is there for you to save and fix. When employees, vendors, contractors, or customers have problems, they ask for your help and you show up to fix it. This is the hero syndrome.

Admittedly, the hero syndrome feels great. It gives a sense of accomplishment and fulfills the desire to be needed. But the hero syndrome is simply not a sustainable way to grow a business. At some point, you will have to stop doing everything yourself and delegate tasks to others. If not, you'll never be able to exit the daily operations of your business and move on to what you really want to do with your life. If you want to work less and to make more – more money, more choices, more freedom, more impact – you'll have to learn to build a foundation for success. You can't make more if you're doing everything yourself.

Both Edward and Cheryl were afflicted with the hero syndrome, Edward more so than Cheryl. Edward lost hundreds of thousands of dollars because of the hero syndrome, but both he *and* Cheryl lost thousands of hours of their lives that could never be regained. By the time the diagnosis arrived, it was too late to make amends–the time was gone and could not be re-lived. Remember: time is a non-renewable resource.

DELEGATION EXPLAINED

What exactly is delegation? Delegation is the act of assigning, entrusting, and empowering someone to act on your behalf. Most people think it is only assigning a task, but that in only one-third of what true delegation is. True delegation also requires that you entrust the task to someone. That means you trust them to do it without looking over their shoulder every five minutes. True delegation also means that you must empower the person to act on your behalf. What does that act of *empowering* mean? In business, it's to give people the tools, resources, technology, training, and encouragement to succeed. They aren't empowered if you don't trust them to do it on their own. Delegation is about training your employees to act for you and as you would act if you were present.

What does delegation look like? There are three very important questions that you need to answer for the person you delegate to. When you answer these three questions, then you are truly delegating, not just assigning a task.

First, when you delegate a task to someone you have to explain to them WHY the task needs to be done in the first place. Many times, the person you delegate to may only think you're giving them a task that you just don't want to do. While at times it's true, that's not actually why that task needs to be done in the first place. There is a reason for that task. It fits somehow into the overall journey of success for the business. Tell them why this task is important. Explain why the task is critical and where it fits into the overall vision of the company. This is the first step in making sure you are truly delegating and not just assigning a task.

Second, you have to make sure they understand HOW to do the task and how to access the resources and tools they're going to need to complete it. You don't have to show them every single step, although with certain technical tasks that may be necessary. But you do need to give them the tools and resources required to accomplish the task. Just knowing why it's important isn't enough. They also must understand how to successfully complete what you've asked them to do, in order for it to be true delegation and not just assigning a task.

Third, you must make sure they understand WHEN the task is due. Imagine for a minute that you delegate a task to a key employee, and this is a recurring task that is due every Wednesday. If the employee doesn't understand that it is due each Wednesday in order to keep a vendor relationship active for example, then the task may not get completed on time and you will lose the relationship with the vendor. It's not enough to explain the why and the how without also explaining the when. Put those three questions together, and you are actually delegating.

Simply assigning someone a task without answering those three questions of why, how, and when, will never get you the freedom that you want. It will just make you have to spend a lot of extra time cleaning up their mess later.

time

WHAT DOES DELEGATION DO FOR YOU?

What you get back from delegation is **time.** Time is the most important resource that any entrepreneur could ever hope to gain more of. *It is finite.* As we've discussed, time is a nonrenewable resource. Once you use it, it's gone forever.

Let's look back at Cherly's story. She sat at the closing table, holding her husband's hand, excited about the life-changing amount of money they were about to receive. However, in that moment, she saw the sorrow in her husband's eyes as they contemplated all the time she had lost while she was building her business over the past decade. No amount of money could make up for that lost time.

Edward was not happy. He was nine months into the earnout period after his sale, and every day he grew more and more frustrated. His job as the CEO of the business – now owned by someone else – was to train his former employees on all of the tasks that Edward used to complete himself. "If I had just done this years ago, I would not have had to be doing this now, in the middle of an earnout. I'd be free," he mumbled to himself.

According to a study conducted by Gail Thomas and revealed in her 2013 book, *The Gift of Time,* 53% of business owners believe that they can grow their business by more than 20% if they delegate 10% of their workload to someone else. That's a big swing! 20% overall growth for offloading a measly 10% of your tasks to someone else? The study revealed that time is the biggest barrier to delegation, yet ironically this is what delegation saves for you. Just like Edward and Cheryl, most entrepreneurs don't delegate because they think it will waste time when they could simply do it faster and better than everyone else. The book went on to reveal that more than a third of business owners believe that they should delegate more even though they don't. Why is that? I believe it's because there is a lot of confusion about what delegation is and how to actually pull it off. Many think they are doing it when they aren't. Let me explain…

DELEGATION IS NOT CONFISCATION

Most hero entrepreneurs practice **confiscation.** Confiscation, unlike delegation, is when you use your authority to lay claim to and separate a task from its holder. In other words, you first relinquish that task to someone else so that they can do it, but then you reclaim it based on your authority and the fact that they aren't performing up to your standards. You haven't delegated anything. Rather, you have confiscated it.

Confiscation will never get your time back, and it will never allow you freedom from the ironic prison of entrepreneurship. This type of "delegation" leads employees to self-sabotaging so that they won't end up having to do it in the future. Think about it: if you regularly confiscate tasks after "delegating" them, then your employees will recognize this pattern. If you assign a task they don't want to do, they will do it wrong so that you will confiscate it back. It's like the husband who doesn't want to wash dishes, so he breaks just enough cups and plates so that his wife will never ask him to do it again. When you practice confiscation rather than true delegation as an entrepreneur, this will hurt them, it will hurt you, and most of all it will hurt your business.

True delegation is not confiscation.

This is what Edward practiced most in his business. Here's one exchange Edward had with an employee early on in the first couple of years of his business.

"Hey, Emma, come here. I want to give you a task." Emma walked over and Edward began to explain what he needed her to do. He went so far as to explain why the task was important, how to do it and when it was due. Emma seemed confident that she could do it, and Edward was satisfied with her attitude and reasonably confident in her abilities.

Emma says: *"Okay, I've got it."* Then, she proceeds to go do the task as Edward had explained – at least the way that she interpreted it.

But all the while, Edward was watching over her shoulder to make sure she was doing everything correctly. Inevitably, she messed up. She did something wrong, and she completed the task in a different way than Edward usually did it. While he watched her closely, he interrupted her process and said: *"Here, let me show you a better way to do it."* Then, he started to involve himself in what she was doing and tried to show her a better method.

Emma then tried to improve a little bit more on what she was doing to please Edward, but she inevitably messed things up again. It wasn't really that bad, it just was a bit different from Edward's customary way of doing things. It's important to note that Emma was not incapable or insufficient. Instead, she simply didn't do it the exact way that Edward did it. Eventually Edward said to her, *"Here. Give that back to me and I'll do it."*

This story repeated itself dozens of times over the first few years of Edward's business. And it wasn't just Emma--it was anyone Edward ever attempted to delegate something to. That was not a true delegation. Instead, it was confiscation. Yes, the words may rhyme, but they are not the same thing. This is because Edward didn't empower Emma to act on his behalf. He didn't entrust her with the task. He gave her a task and expected her to perform it with perfection, the way he did. Edward simply did not empower her by giving her the specific training, resources, and time necessary to accomplish her tasks, so of course she was not able to finish the job. Emma also never understood the reason why she had to complete the task in the first place.

In order for Edward to have truly delegated this task to Emma, he should have made sure she understood *why* she was responsible for doing what she was doing. *What's the larger purpose? What are we trying to accomplish here? Why is this necessary? What's the process?* If Emma had been able to fully understand what Edward was trying to accomplish, she likely could have figured out better ways to accomplish the task, and Edward wouldn't be stuck in the middle of a three-year earnout right now.

DELEGATION IS NOT ABDICATION

Granted, not all entrepreneurs practice confiscation. However, those who are not doing this are practicing something else that also rhymes with delegation – *abdication.*

Abdication is when you formally separate yourself or divest yourself from the responsibility of a task. It is like relinquishing or renouncing the throne that is rightfully yours. Entrepreneurs who practice this end up assigning tasks and never check back to see how things went. Sometimes it works out when you abdicate, because the person you give the task to will do a great job. Unfortunately though, more times than not, the person that you assign that task to simply doesn't know how to do it and you don't know if they did it right until things start collapsing.

Abdication was Cheryl's favorite form of delegation. Here's one exchange Cheryl had with an employee early on in the first couple of years of her business.

"Hey, Bob, come here. I have something for you to do. I need you to do this for me." Bob came into her office, and Cheryl proceeded to tell Bob what needed to be done. Cheryl was diligent to explain why she was asking Bob to do it and why it was important. She even explained to him the best practices for completing the task and showed him some of the software he could use to do it. Finally, she explained the deadline for the task. It was an ongoing assignment that was due every 30 days and was critical to the overall technology infrastructure they were building as a company.

Bob gave her a confident smile and thanked her for the opportunity. He assured her, *"I won't let you down, boss!"* They shook hands and Bob walked out of her office.

Six months later, Cheryl noticed that the recurring orders on some of their best-selling products had flatlined. *What happened?* After a bit of investigating, she discovered that the software updates she had assigned to Bob six months ago that were part of the recurring order automations were not working at all. She had abdicated this task to Bob, and he had screwed up. They lost tens of thousands of dollars in revenue, not to mention the bad reviews that resulted from customers not receiving their orders as expected.

When she confronted Bob, he explained that as far as he could tell, everything was working fine. After all, he didn't have insight into the financial reports like Cheryl did, so from his perspective nothing seemed amiss. She blamed herself for this mistake, not Bob. Cheryl learned the hard way that delegation and abdication aren't the same thing. This abdication stunt she pulled with Bob cost her a lot of money.

Of course, abdication is easier than confiscation, but it's still not delegation. Abdication is the act of giving up authority as well as the responsibility for the outcome of a task. As the entrepreneur and founder, you have full control and authority. Therefore, you must accept responsibility for all of the situational outcomes, no matter who does the task. It all comes back to you, in every circumstance. When Cheryl "delegated" that task to Bob, the outcome still fell under her responsibility, but she wasn't paying attention. She didn't fully delegate. By the time she realized this, it was too late.

You will only be able to emancipate yourself from the ironic prison of entrepreneurship by practicing the art of true delegation.

Overall, a good founder delegates appropriately and accepts responsibility for the outcome, without meddling in the daily activities of these tasks, while also pushing forward to make sure that the outcome hits the objective. Delegation is about setting up your team to carry out tasks in your absence, the same way that you would perform them if you were present.

Think about it like this: on one side, there's a pendulum that swings out towards abdication. This is where we give up and don't ever think about the tasks at hand. We give everything to somebody else and never go back to check on things. The other extreme is where the pendulum swings in the opposite direction, which is where we confiscate. This is when we delegate, but then we take the task back into our own hands because we don't like how they're doing it.

STOP FEARING THE DIP

Why do we do this? Why do so many hero entrepreneurs practice confiscation instead of true delegation. Why do others practice full-on abdication? The reason this occurs is because we don't think we'll be able to survive the dip. *What is the dip?* From our examples above, Emma and Bob are not the dip. Of course, you might have an occasional employee who's a dip, but that's not what we're talking about in this instance. The "dip" is what can happen in terms of productivity and outcome. For example, if you are completing a certain task that you've been working on since you started your company, you are used to the final outcomes that you provide. As far as you are concerned, you do it at 100%. As you do that task and get a certain outcome every single time, it starts to become predictable. You know what will happen, but it still requires your time, attention, energy, and resources.

When you delegate that task to someone else as Edward and Cheryl did, the person you delegate to will not do it the way you do. Emma won't get it done as fast. Bob will think he's doing great when he's actually failing. Neither will follow the exact same steps you would have, had you done it yourself. In fact, the outcome might even look a little bit different. That dip in outcome or productivity is something that most entrepreneurs who have hero syndrome cannot stand. They don't like to see the dip, nor do they think that they can survive it.

What happens if Emma does it wrong and we get two weeks behind on this project as a result? Honestly, that's fine. I would rather be two weeks behind on a project than have to constantly be the person that has to get everything done. In the long run, that two-week delay in getting the project across the finish line isn't going to make a tremendous difference or cause a loss of income in most cases. Instead, what it will do is give Emma the valuable experience of running a project on her own and learning how to do that task successfully and independently. Even though she doesn't do it to your standard yet, she will eventually be able to do this task better than you. That's a fact, even though you don't see it yet.

What if Bob completely misses the mark and we lose tens of thousands of dollars? Again, while not optimal, you can survive this just like Cheryl did. It hurts, but it won't kill you. If she had checked in and delegated appropriately, the outcome would have been totally different.

From the time when you delegate the task, to the time that the productivity boost happens, know that there will be a dip – but also know that you'll survive. Conceptually, this is what delegation is all about.

As I said earlier, James embraced delegation from the beginning. Here's one exchange he had with an employee early on in his business.

"Hey, Justin, come here. I have something for you to do. You're just the guy for the job." Justin and James met in the conference room, and James explained what he needed from Justin. He took the time to not only tell Justin why he was asking Justin to do it and why it was important, but he also explained where this task fit into the overall vision of the company. *"You see, when this task is completed correctly and on time, our customers have a much better experience that leads to more repeat business. Keeping a customer is easier and more profitable than trying to get a new one. Does that make sense?"*

Justin listened intently as James even explained to him the best practices for completing the task and showed him some of the resources and technology he could use to do it. Finally, James explained the deadline for the task, saying that it was something that needed to be completed each and every day before closing.

"I got it, boss," said Justin. *"I'll get started right away."*

James replied, *"Before you get started, I want you to know that this is a trial delegation period. I only need you to do this for thirty days to see how it works out. You and I will meet each Thursday morning at 9:00 for 15–20 minutes to see how things are going. Otherwise, you can ask me questions any time. I trust you will do a great job. You're an important team member, and this is an important task. Thanks for doing this."* After James said all of that, they shook hands and went on with the rest of their day.

What James knew that both Edward and Cheryl didn't was that there's a certain way to delegate that assures success. That last statement James made to Justin set them both up for success, and it paid off handsomely for James when he was ready to exit the daily operations of his business.

I'm going to reveal the finer points of this delegation method used by James at the end of this chapter, but before I do, I want to share a theory that helps drive home the concept of why delegation is so important to begin with.

MARGIN THEORY

Let me introduce you to something called Margin Theory. Personally, I didn't know about Margin Theory until I started working on my PhD in business a few years ago. Margin Theory was one of the most important things that I learned and still use very often today. It has become a core concept in my coaching practice. As a matter of fact, it is the only thing I took away from my doctoral studies. In case you're wondering, I never finished my PhD. Once I learned this concept, I was good to go. There was no reason to continue – it was that instrumental!

Originally, the concept was developed by a sociologist named Howard Yale McClusky. His specialty was gerontology, which is the study of elderly people. To put it in a very crass way, he was trying to find the answer to a question we've all heard: *Can you teach an old dog new tricks? Do older people have the capacity to learn new tasks and do new things?*

What he discovered was something very specific to "margin." While the way he studied margin had nothing to do with business, I was able to see a connection between what he studied in sociology and my own world of business and entrepreneurship.

Let's talk about what the margin is actually referring to. First of all, the secret here is that margin is where all of the success happens. It's the place from which you're able to exit without exiting. Margin is the space in which you're able to get that idea of "more" that you want in your life. Whether that relates to more choices, more time, more freedom or more impact – this is the place where that all happens. It's also the word that we refer to when talking about space, like the blank space bordering a written or printed area on a page. It's the same as the margins of this page you're reading right now.

There is an interesting reason why margins were put in books to begin with. In the 1400s, the printing press was invented by Johannes Gutenberg and books started to be printed. The press would print the words all the way to the edges of the paper. Top to bottom, right to left. The problem with doing this and taking up every ounce of space on the page is that any time the book was handled or shipped, any damage that occurred would normally happen on the edges. While a book was in transit, the edges of the book might get banged; while a book was in storage, mice or rats may nibble the edges of the pages of the book to satisfy their hunger. Over time, the actual words around the edges of the pages would slowly disappear, and with that, also the meaning of the text. Imagine opening a book and not being able to read the whole story because some of the sentences have gone missing around the edges.

The solution to this problem? Margins. Printers introduced margins into books in order to preserve the writing and make it possible for the pages to endure wear and tear over time. Margins give a little extra space in the event that something unexpected or negative happens. Beyond printers and publishing, margins serve essentially the same purpose in life and business. They make a particular thing possible, such as an extra amount of money or time that allows for dealing with emergencies. It's that spare amount of measure or degree allowed for contingencies or unexpected situations.

Most importantly, margin is the thing that most entrepreneurs are lacking, yet it is where true success finally happens. The exit lifestyle is a life lived with plenty of margin. Most entrepreneurs don't have margin because they're not delegating. They're doing everything themselves. They don't have any margin. There's no extra space for them to deal with unexpected emergencies. Just like the words on the pages of the old printing press books, they are spread to every edge of their businesses, from top to bottom and left to right. When this happens, there's absolutely zero room for error. *So then what happens if you get hurt or sick? What happens if, like those books, you get banged up or frayed around the edges for one reason or another? What's the buffer? Where's your margin?*

In McClusky's study of Margin Theory and the elderly, he found the only way they could learn new tasks is if they had margin. And margin, he discovered, was the ratio based on relative amounts of **power** and **load**. This concept is extremely important. He discovered that balance is needed in life between work and the amount of energy available to do the work. That's where this ratio of power and load start to come in.

So how does all of this actually work?

Load is anything that dissipates energy. Load is everything you have to do at any given time. Load is infinite.

If you were to take a piece of paper out right now and write down everything that constitutes "load" in your life and business, how long would that list be? Go ahead and do that: create a "Load List." Don't leave anything out. Here are some examples from the "Load Lists" that my clients have created over the years:

- Scheduling meetings
- Producing financial reports
- Running sales calls
- Meeting with vendors
- Hiring and firing employees
- Verifying that tasks were done on time
- Meeting with prospects
- Meetings with bankers and lawyers
- Checking emails
- Attending Zoom meetings or conference calls
- Getting continuing education credits
- Calling back a customer who had a complaint
- Updating the website
- Posting on social media

The list can go on and on. What is on your "Load List" as an entrepreneur? To decrease your load, you must "offload" (i.e., "delegate") tasks as much as possible. "Margin may be increased by reducing Load or increasing Power," said McClusky. Since that is true, one half of actually attaining margin in our lives is offloading as much as possible. This will by default increase our margin, but we cannot only pay attention to the load side of the ratio; we must also pay attention to the power side of the ratio.

Power is the ability to deal effectively with load. "Power" is anything that gives us energy and the ability to accomplish tasks. "Power" is finite, so do not take it for granted.

There are two ways we can get power in our lives: directly and indirectly. For example, we can get direct power by hiring a mentor, coach, or consultant. Working with these professionals will help us get more mental power. Another way to get power directly is by joining coaching programs, cohorts, and masterminds. Don't underestimate the skills you can receive through these groups. Some of the most successful entrepreneurs in the world attribute their success to the power of a mastermind.

Direct power is the best and most potent kind of power that we can receive in our lives, but there is a lot of value in indirect power as well. For example, you can get indirect power by reading books like this one. Even though you and I aren't working directly together, you are increasing your power indirectly through the content in this book. If you want to compound the power that this book contains, you can do the activities I recommend throughout the book and increase your power tenfold. It's not only books that can indirectly give you power, but you can also listen to podcasts, audiobooks, or watch instructional videos on YouTube. Each of these ways are wonderful methods of increasing your mental power as an entrepreneur.

NOTE: I invite you to connect with my content more deeply if you are interested in increasing your power indirectly through my free content. My podcast, The Root of All Success, can be heard on any podcast platform, or you can watch the episodes on YouTube. Go to therootofallsuccess.com/podcast to learn more. I also host a live webinar series called The Entrepreneur Masters Series twice a month, which is curated and designed especially for entrepreneurs. It is a 90-minute masterclass with guest experts on important topics like finance, sales, marketing, investing, leadership, and more. Go to therealjasonduncan.com/ems and register for the next episode. It's completely free and a great way to get power.

Remember, you can increase your margin in life by either decreasing load, increasing power, or both. I recommend doing both!

Load is represented as L. Power is represented as P. Margin is M.

If you want margin if your life, you want your power/load ratio to look like this:

P > L = M

This reads: "If power is greater than load, that equals margin."

If you feel like you have no margin and you are running around all the time, your power/load ratio looks like this:

$$P < L \neq M$$

This reads: "If power is less than load, that equals no margin."

In the power/load ratio, if P is greater than L, that equals margin. Having margin means you can deal with the extra thing that might arise. However, if your power/load ratio has P less than L, that means you don't have margin. What McClusky discovered in his study was that with the elderly people who were trying to learn new tasks, if they were overloaded or over-stimulated, their brains could not function efficiently enough to learn. In this case, they had no margin to help them deal with anything new. On the other hand, if you put them into a calmer setting where the load was reduced, they were able to have more power to learn new things. The removal of taxing loads provided them with the margin needed so that they were able to learn new things.

APPLYING MARGIN THEORY TO YOUR BUSINESS

I know it doesn't sound like there would necessarily be a larger business application here, but think about this for a minute. As an entrepreneur, load is infinite. Load has the capacity to fully dissipate your energy. As we defined it earlier, load is anything and everything that you have to do at any given time, which can be endless.

The upside is that load *can* be reduced. When you reduce load, you in turn increase your margin. I want you to think about this again. *What's on your load list today?* If you were to write down everything that's going on in your life as a business owner right this very moment, what would be on your list? Of course, there are going to be meetings and proposals that need to be prepared. There will be employees that need to be hired, fired, and reviewed.

There's also the real estate element, or the building that you're renting. Issues and challenges with your technology services can come into play. Taxes need to be taken into consideration. Banking and financial needs that need to be handled. Your load likely includes innumerable other projects that you're working on.

Here's the thing: that load list must be parallel to your personal ability to deal with it. This is where delegation comes into play, as it is one of the best ways to deal specifically with load. That's why it's the very first core principle for exiting successfully. Once you have knowledge and awareness of your load list, you can take the list and start delegating some of those tasks to other people.

ACTION STEP: I want you to stop reading this book for a moment and write down your **"Load List."** Go back and review the examples I shared to help you get started. *What are the things on your list that you're doing on a daily, weekly, or monthly basis that create load? What tasks are dissipating your energy? What elements of your business can you delegate?* Then, write down how you are regularly receiving power in your life, which is your **"Power List."** *Do you have a business coach? Are you part of a mastermind? Have you ever enrolled in a course or program that will help you get more power as an entrepreneur?* If you have no power to deal with the energy required to handle the load, then you'll never be able to position yourself in a place of success. When you have a large task at hand, you must structure things specifically and use your time in a way that allows you to handle the current load that you're dealing with.

BECOMING A MASTER DELEGATOR

James was a master delegator, and it was the first key he used to unlock the exit lifestyle for himself. Remember the conversation James had with Justin earlier? The last statement James made to Justin is where master delegators shine, and I'm about to reveal the method James used to become a master delegator.

Ultimately, creating space to handle load and to make a specific margin for yourself is where true success happens. That's where James was able to exit. As I defined it earlier, margin is the space where exiting can occur… when you choose to do so. If you create margin through delegation, your business learns to survive without you being in the mix 100% of the time. When you embrace delegation like James did, you stop handling everything on your own. And when you exit, things will not fall apart. Delegation increases your power and decreases your load at the same time – it's addition by subtraction. By delegating, you're literally offloading things to other people so that you're able to pay attention to the most important tasks of setting the vision, communicating the vision, and building the asset. This also permits you to exit easily when you are ready. It's completely necessary.

Here are the six steps James used to become a master delegator:

Step 1 to Master Delegation

Using the "Load List" you just made as your reference, make a "Top 10 List" of things you must complete at any given time that are important to the business – but not critical. These are things that you currently do alone but things that someone else could do. Be honest and take off the hero cape. Go ahead make your top 10 list now.

Step 2 to Master Delegation

Next, choose one item from the list and delegate it to someone else for 30 days. Remember what we talked about earlier: delegation is the act of assigning, entrusting, and empowering someone else to act on your behalf. You need to make sure they understand what the task is, why they're doing it, how to do it, and when it is due. That is delegating, not just assigning.

Step 3 to Master Delegation

Set aside a time to check in on their progress, but only once a week. No more and no less. For example, when James delegated that task to Justin, he told him that they'd have a check-in meeting every Thursday at 9:00 AM. The time was set, and therefore

James didn't need to check in with Justin every single day. If James had checked in every day (like Edward did with Emma), he would have run the risk of confiscating that task back from him. On the other hand, if James had not checked in with Justin at all (like Cheryl did with Bob), he would have run the risk of abdicating the task. The once-a-week check-in keeps you and the person you delegate the task to on track, allowing the wheels of delegation to turn at the right speed and in the right direction.

Step 4 to Master Delegation

Step four is the hardest. This is the step that separates successful entrepreneurs who are able to exit without exiting, from the ones who are forever trapped in the ironic prison of entrepreneurship. This is the moment when you actually do your check-in, where you are only allowed to offer praise and not allowed to correct. That's right. No corrections are allowed. You need to look for ways to praise the person's work but not to make it better! The Law of Discovery tells us that we all learn more from what we experience on our own than what we're told. Toddlers don't always learn that candles are hot from their moms and dads telling them this information. At some point, they have to burn their fingers before they will truly learn. The same thing is true for employees who are learning new tasks within your business. Sometimes they have to fail in order to learn how to succeed. If you're going to learn how to delegate, you can only praise their own work. You can't correct it or try to fix it yourself. Here's what that looks like.

James meets Justin at 9:00 AM on Thursdays for their weekly check in. They sit down at the conference room table and James says, *"How's everything going?"*

Justin gives a report on what's been happening, and James realizes that Justin has messed up. Unfortunately, he's not doing his task correctly. But unless Justin's failure is causing imminent danger to a human being, creating a legal issue that could make legitimate trouble down the road, or starting a financial disaster, James simply needs to let him fail. And that's exactly what he does in this scenario. James' job is not to correct him – instead, it's to look for things that Justin has done right and give him praise for that.

For instance, if Justin comes in and he's done something out of order but was very organized in the way he did it, James could say, *"Okay, good. Thank you for letting me know what's going on. I really appreciate you being very organized in this task. That means a lot. At the end of the 30 days, we'll review how it all went. For right now, just keep going and stay organized. Is there anything you think I would do differently if I had been doing this task instead of you?"*

That last question is important. It should allow Justin to reflect on any disparity between what he's done and how his boss would have done it. James is careful not to offer unsolicited corrections or advice, but rather allows Justin to analyze the situation and self-correct. At this point, Justin is given the opportunity to think deeply about how he's been doing things as compared to the way he thinks his boss would have done it. They discuss. James still doesn't offer any corrective instructions unless Justin asks a specific question. If Justin asks questions, James obviously needs to answer those questions but without correcting him. The point here is that master delegators don't try to make things better. Instead, they just need to praise the person for the good work they have accomplished and give them space to fail and succeed.

Step 5 to Master Delegation

Step five is almost as difficult as step four. This is called "The 80% Rule." Once the person you delegate to is able to do a task at 80% of your output, you can permanently mark that off of your list of personal tasks. You aren't looking for perfection, as that will come much later. At this point in the delegation process, you are simply looking for 80%. Eventually, they will do the task as good or better than you, but not yet. You must understand that this dip in productivity is not permanent.

Some would argue that you could walk away from that task forever if the person is able to perform it at 50% of your ability.

However, I believe that it's 80%. Fifty percent means that the task is being executed wrong half the time, and that's not good enough.

Let me give you an example from my own experience with one of my employees. Ricky started working with me right out of graduate school. At the time, he didn't know much about our business but was very interested in the energy industry. He was eager to learn, and I hired him to handle some of the operational things that were going on in the business. Until that point, I'd handled 100% of those operational duties. I had been doing all of the lighting audits. Every week, I would order all of the equipment and schedule all the installations. I'd coordinate with the customers and with the vendors and then do the shipping and POs. Essentially, I did it all.

When Ricky started, I delegated those tasks to him. He was not very good at performing them at first – *but he was good enough.* At some point in his training, he leveled up and started doing about 80% of my output. After that, I never looked back. I let him continue to carry out that task full-time without my interference.

Today, Ricky is much better at all those tasks than I am or ever was. This is because that's all that he does. He doesn't have the role of a CEO who has to run every aspect of the business like I did for so many years. He only has to manage the operations, and that is now his area of expertise. When you're learning how to delegate and you get to step 5, you're now simply asking the person to do 80% of your output. Not 100%. Don't let perfection become the enemy of the good.

As another example, I have a client named Landon who's an attorney. He went through my 10-Hour Entrepreneur coaching program a few years ago. Like most attorneys, when he started his practice, he was the only attorney there. This is the case for many expert technicians, such as doctors, lawyers, CPAs, chiropractors, and dentists, where they are the single practitioner. In many cases they aren't entrepreneurs and don't have much business experience at all. Landon had started his own firm several years earlier, and he was still the only guy. He was doing everything necessary to run all the aspects of his own business.

After taking my 10-Hour Entrepreneur coaching program, he decided to hire two associate attorneys to work in his firm. They were fresh out of law school and looking for their first big opportunity. Landon knew he needed to hire more people, or he would never be able to exit his firm. He also knew he had to delegate a lot of the tasks of finding new clients, handling clients, writing drafts of proposals, documents and contracts. Not long after he hired the new associates, I ran into all three of them at a local cigar club in Nashville. Landon was excited to introduce me to them. He was very proud that they were on staff with him and that they were part of his business.

We met privately later on so he could tell me how things were going. What he had discovered after hiring them and delegating tasks was that he now was able to spend more time going out and finding higher profile clients. Not only that, but he was also able to bill their rate at his old rate and raise his rate to a higher hourly fee. This is because now he was seen as the main attorney in the firm – not just the *only* attorney in the firm. In my coaching program, Landon learned how to embrace delegation so that he's now working less on the old tasks. He's able to make more money per hour, while having more hours per week billed, because he has three people rather than just himself. If he'd expected others to perform at 100% of his output, this would have never happened and he'd still be a single practitioner with no margin.

Step 6 to Master Delegation

The final step to becoming a master delegator is to repeat this process every 30 days until all noncritical tasks are off your list. It won't take you long to go through your entire list, because once you get the hang of delegating a task or two, you will then be able to delegate as many as three to five tasks at a time without worrying about the outcome like you used to.

If you follow these six steps to delegation, you will learn how to do this effectively, and you will become a master delegator like James in no time. Remember that margin comes from having more power than load. You can delegate these tasks, which will decrease your load and thereby increase your margin. Not only that, but it will also start to increase your overall profit margin, which is the type of margin I don't have to explain to you. At first there may be a dip, but eventually, it will start to increase. Stay the course!

DELEGATING TO TECHNOLOGY

Before I move to the next core principle in Chapter 7, I want to mention another method of delegation that many people overlook, which is delegating to technology.

Again, delegation is offloading tasks. So far, we've discussed this process only in relation to delegating specific tasks to other people and mainly employees. However, you can also delegate tasks and operations to the power of technology. In today's world, there's a vast array of tools and platforms that you can employ to assist you. In my 10-Hour Entrepreneur course, I dive into how you can use a few simple pieces of technology in your daily life. These are things that have helped me to save dozens of hours every single week.

One of those pieces of technology is Calendly. As entrepreneurs, one of the things on our load list is scheduling meetings. We have to schedule meetings, attend meetings, and go to meetings all the time. The act of scheduling sometimes takes hours to figure out. I used to send out emails that said: *"Hey, I'm available during these times next week."* Then, it can take 24 or 48 hours for the person I have invited to respond. By the time they've chosen a time, I've already booked that time with someone else, so we have to start all over again. Calendly is a scheduling tool that makes this process so much more efficient by effectively offloading scheduling from your schedule. Check out Calendly at *calendly.com*.

Another app I love to use is Dubb. As an entrepreneur, communicating with your clients and prospects in a way that gets attention is hard to do. Also, writing emails is a time-consuming task that steals hours from your day. Imagine being able to send your prospects a video email instead! That's one of the tricks of using Dubb. It tracks the opens, the clicks, and the watch time so you know when and if the person you sent the email to actually saw your message or not. Not only that but Dubb has a full suite of CRM and follow-up tools that can save you lots of time. It's another secret weapon I use to delegate simple tasks that would otherwise weigh me down every day. If you want to get a free trial and a huge discount on Dubb, use my affiliate link here: *therealjasonduncan.com/dubb*.

A third and final technology that saves me hours of time each week is Storyy. Thirty years ago, you weren't in business unless you had an ad in the yellow pages. Ten years ago, no one took you seriously unless your business had a website. Today, if you want to succeed in business you have to be posting videos on social media. The problem is that you often don't know what to say or how to edit the video. Additionally, you certainly don't have time to write the captions, create the hashtags, and post the video to each platform. That's the beauty of delegating these tasks to Storyy. The platform handles everything for you. I use them for all of my social media content, and they do an absolutely amazing job. Remember, delegation is not just about *delegating tasks to people*… sometimes it's about delegating to *technology* like Storyy. If you want to try Storyy and get a great discount, use my affiliate link here: *therealjasonduncan.com/storyy*.

There are so many apps that can do administrative tasks for you and your team. This takes away many items from your everyday to do list, which can save you an immense amount of time and money. This also reduces your load and allows you to have the time and resources to do more of what you want to do. If you can find software or technology that can save you time for the cost of a few dollars a year, spend that money. Remember, if you leverage money for time, you're doing the right thing. Stop trying to leverage your time to save money – that's the wrong way.

DELEGATING TO VIRTUAL ASSISTANTS

There are also virtual assistants (VAs) that work for you either virtually or remotely. They're not located physically where you are and can easily be in another part of the country or even somewhere overseas. I have successfully used VAs in four or five different countries who've each helped me do everything from social media, to video editing, to writing, to scheduling, to research, to administrative assistance, to billing, to literally anything that an in-office employee could do. Right now, I use a few different virtual assistants in the Philippines, Bangladesh, and Uganda to do various tasks for me. There are many platforms available, but one I'm partial to is *VirtualStaff.ph,* which is a Philippines-based company. VAs in the Philippines are great, because English is their primary language, which makes communication much better. *VirtualStaff.ph* and these kinds of platforms are designed so that you can hire a VA on an ongoing basis. Go to *virtualstaff.ph* to learn more.

If you simply need a project completed, such as a logo design, website update, copywriting, or similar work, I recommend a freelance service like Fiverr or Upwork. With these, you can browse thousands of VAs who are looking for single-project gigs. Typically, these professionals work for around $5 per project. Often, the project may cost more, but the point is that you can delegate tasks to other people through platforms like Fiverr or Upwork for pennies on the dollar and in a way that will also save you a lot of time instead of you doing the project yourself. Fiverr has a great affiliate program that gives the clients that I send $100 off their first gig. To use my affiliate link go to *therealjasonduncan.com/fiverr*.

Part of my coaching program shows you exactly how to use

virtual assistants, where to find them, how to hire them, onboard them, and use them on a daily basis. The other interesting thing about using a VA is they typically cost a fraction of what a part-time or full-time employee would, and they provide services that are just as good. Of course, it is always up to you to run a hiring process that screens potential VAs in the same way you'd run a process to hire someone to work in your office. As with hiring anyone, make sure you hire slow and fire fast – you can read more on this concept in Chapter 9. If you're interested in learning how to employ a virtual assistant, check out my 10-Hour Entrepreneur course at *ExitWithoutExiting.com*.

CONCLUSION

The first core principle in figuring out how to exit without exiting so you can live the exit lifestyle is "Embrace Delegation." If you commit to practicing the true art of delegation within your business – not confiscating or abdicating – within 90 days, you will find yourself rising above the weeds of daily operations. You will begin to feel a sense of freedom and fulfillment as you see your business flourish, without having to be the hero at every turn. Your employees will begin to feel empowered and perform at higher levels than ever before. Once they know you trust them and that they see the vision you have for the company, along with their role in realizing that vision, they will exceed all of your expectations. Re-read this chapter as often as necessary to become a master delegator.

7. ELIMINATE STRESS

Let's take a look back at Edward and his principles for managing stress. Unfortunately, Edward always seemed stressed out to those who knew him best. He was very busy and very few days passed when he had enough time to get the things done that were on his to do list. This was very normal for Edward. His wife and family had gotten used to this. On the rare occasion when Edward was relaxed, she wondered if everything was ok. His employees didn't know any better either. To them, the owner of the business was always supposed to be working. Inadvertently, Edward had trained his employees to think and believe that "busy-ness" was normal, acceptable, and a sign of success for the average entrepreneur. They watched him, and their actions began to emulate his own. His stress levels ended up rubbing off on the entire company, and it showed. Customers noticed that Edward and his team always seemed on edge. Details were missed from time to time. Deadlines caused even higher levels of stress, and customers who didn't like stress eventually moved their business to other vendors who seemed easier to get along with and do business with. Unknowingly, the stress that Edward lived in and accepted as "normal" lost him a lot of potential revenue. Ultimately, it was one of the reasons that the only way he could exit his business was through an earnout.

In the previous chapter, we discussed delegation, which is the first core strategy when it comes to being able to exit without exiting. Now, I want to tell you everything you need to know about stress management so you don't end up like Edward. Oddly enough, stress and delegation go hand in hand. The less you delegate, the more stress you typically feel. The more you delegate, the less stress you have.

Also, please note the title of this chapter uses the word "eliminate" rather than "manage." I believe that stress can be totally eliminated from your life with the tools I'm going to share with you in this chapter. It's not about managing stress – it's about eliminating it altogether. Once you learn how stress is caused and what to do with it when it arises, you can get rid of it. Trust me.

Before I dive into eliminating stress as a core strategy, I want to discuss something that I typically talk to my clients about at this point in our conversation: the difference between rhythm and routine. As an addendum to Chapter 6, you can think of this as yet another way to gain power.

RHYTHM VERSUS ROUTINE

Let's talk about the difference between rhythm and routine. A lot of people look at routines and how they will make you successful, like if you have certain things you do in the morning and throughout the day in order to add some structure. While I'm good with all of that, the reality is that routines don't work for everybody. Some people (like me) don't do well with that set structure. They feel like routines are restrictions that can lead to guilt if not upheld religiously. Maybe that's you, too. Instead, people like us are more efficient with *rhythm.* What's the actual difference?

Let's first look at routine. A routine is a set of customary or unchanging – and often mechanically performed – activities or procedures. Some routines are good and healthy, while others can be damaging due to legalism. Legalism is when we set a specific standard for the purpose of exalting ourselves above other people. For example, there are many gurus who have YouTube channels, videos, and books on how you must get up at 5:00 AM if you're going to be successful. Some routine-pushers will tell you to take cold showers. They tell you to start doing this routine or that routine in order to plan out your day in the most efficient manner. While those routines probably do work for some, the problem with people espousing all the benefits of routines is that they have turned their particular routine into a legalistic way of doing things. In other words: *"If you don't do it, you're not going to be as good as me."*

I can't tell you how many entrepreneurs I've run into that talk about how they're part of the "5:00 AM club." When they ask me if I am, they're surprised to hear that I don't even set an alarm, because I've designed my life to operate around rhythms rather than routines.

What exactly is a rhythm? This is a regular movement or a pattern of movements that become part of your everyday activity. It's essentially a sequence of any recurring functions or events, such as certain physiological functions of the body like your cardiac rhythm (i.e., your heartbeat). Rhythms give us the foundational beat to which life should operate. Some people do very well within routines, and they need them. They know that if they get up at 5:00 AM every single day, exercise, and do whatever they need to do before work – such as making coffee, doing breathing exercises, meditating, and journaling – they'll be more productive. But for other people like me, committing to a routine and then falling out of it makes me feel genuinely guilty. I start believing that I'm not living up to the standard that I *should* be, and it throws my whole day off.

Instead of routines, I choose to live my life by rhythms. For example, my morning rhythm begins with waking up whenever my body decides it's time, which is usually between 5:30 AM and 6:30 AM every morning. I roll out of bed directly onto my knees and say a quick prayer, thanking Jesus for being my King and thanking Him for a good night's sleep in a warm bed. Then I get into my workout gear. I ride my bicycle and workout with my TRX straps. Next, I make a pot of decaf coffee and eat a protein bar. While drinking coffee and eating breakfast, I do some reading, and then work through my daily prayers and affirmations on my phone, using an app called PrayerMate *(www.prayermate.net)*. Next, I check in on my social media feeds just to see what's going on, and then reply to comments and questions that may have been posted to my feed overnight. *(You can connect with me on Instagram and/or LinkedIn under: @therealjasonduncan)* After about a half hour or so, I get up, shower, get dressed, and move on with my day.

Because I've committed to a life of rhythm rather than routine, guilt doesn't get to me when my morning rhythm is interrupted for some reason. It's true that I feel the effects of not being able to go through the motions in the morning if I'm unable to do so for some reason. However, I don't feel guilty for not doing it. For example, I have one morning each week when I meet with a friend for coffee. Today was that day – I got up, showered and dressed, and then went straight to the coffee shop to meet my friend. Afterward, I went to the chiropractor. This coffee meeting with my friend interrupted my usual morning rhythm, but it's actually part of a weekly rhythm that I enjoy very much. Because I'm not tied into a certain daily routine, I am able to keep my rhythm without getting upset with myself for missing a particular, mechanically performed activity. If I cannot go through my normal rhythms in the same place and time each day, I'll find another time when I can work them in. For example, today when I went to the chiropractor after coffee, I found myself going through my prayer list while lying on the chiropractor's decompression machine for 15 minutes after my adjustment.

If you're not a routine person, just know that you can have rhythms in your life – certain things that happen on a regularly occurring basis – without being committed to a rigid routine. On the other hand, it's also great if you're a routine person. Just continue committing to that routine if it helps you with productivity and makes you feel good about yourself. Either way– whether you're a routine person or a rhythm person – the point is to make sure that you have **power**. Don't allow the legalistic routines set by other people to cause you stress simply because you cannot adhere to their version of a perfect day. Do whatever works for you, because if you don't, you'll end up adding more stress to your life. Stress drains your power, and with it, your productivity and ability to do more. Let's look into this more closely.

THE LAW OF OPEN CYCLES

If I am committed to staying with my rhythm on a regular basis, my stress levels remain almost completely nonexistent. When I get out of rhythm for a while, the stress begins to creep back in, as I'm not "closing cycles" in the correct way. Open cycles can make such an impact, though they're not something that many people have even heard about. In any case, they are directly related to your daily stress levels. Let me explain.

Stress can have a wide-ranging effect on our overall mood and behavioral patterns. It can cause irritability, anxiety, depression, headaches, and insomnia. These are some of the symptoms that arise in people who have chronic stress, which can lead to even more serious issues over time. It's so important to eliminate stress from your life and from your business atmosphere as you prepare to exit. If not, you'll never be able to actually leave the business. Stress will undeniably keep you tied to the business, because like we talked about in the last chapter, the hero syndrome will make you think that you can overcome the stress just by showing up and doing the work. Unfortunately, that's not true.

Contrary to popular opinion, the single greatest cause of stress in the human condition does not come from the endurance of stressful situations, but rather from having too many open cycles at one time. This is what the Law of Open Cycles teaches us. That begs the question: *what exactly is an open cycle?* An open cycle is anything that has a start, a change, and a stop. This could refer to a task, a relationship, a project, or regular correspondence like a piece of mail or a text message. An open cycle is basically anything that will eventually be written on your to-do list – but they are not *only* to-do list items, as you will see.

Let's look at an example to illustrate the effect of open cycles on our brains. Assume you arrive at your office on a Monday morning, and you turn on your computer for the first time that week. Throughout the day, you open up various applications on your computer and tabs on your Internet browser. If you're anything like me, by the end of the day, you have dozens of tabs and applications open. I often ask this question during my coaching program: *"How many applications and tabs would be open on your computer at the end of a Monday if you did NOT close any of them after opening them?"* People often answer between 20 and 50. Some will even say between 50 and 100! That's a lot of tabs.

Now, let's say you go home after work on Monday and never shut your computer down. You don't close any tabs, you don't exit out of any apps – you leave everything open. On Tuesday morning, you go to work and do the same thing. You continue to open new tabs and applications. Maybe you don't open as many on Tuesday because you're still going to reuse some from the day before, but now you add a few more. On Wednesday and Thursday, you do the same thing. Remember, you still haven't closed anything. Every tab and every application you've opened since Monday morning is still open.

When Friday afternoon rolls around, you have so many apps open that it becomes a bit overwhelming. Think about how well your computer is running at this point. It has probably become very slow, because your RAM can't keep up with all of the open tabs and applications. Unfortunately, if you do that too often, you end up getting the spinning pinwheel of death on the screen. Your computer freezes up, and you have to turn it off and turn it back on to reboot everything. When your computer starts back up, what happens? You've lost several of the things you were working on, because you didn't save them.

The same thing happens on your phone. If you go through the whole day or even a whole week without ever shutting your phone off, closing tabs, or shutting down applications, your battery will begin to drain extremely fast. The percentage of battery life remaining will drop by the second, and you will have to rush to find a charger to keep your phone from outright dying while you finish your tasks. Your phone gets hot, starts to lag, and may even freeze up and become unresponsive.

Your brain works the same way. When there are so many tabs and applications opened up – as we refer to as "open cycles" (i.e., tasks and things on your brain all at once) you can't focus on anything. The more you open, the more stress you feel. As we discussed, this is exactly what an open cycle amounts to, and your brain can only handle so many of them. For example, one of the open cycles in your life right now is that you're reading this book. You've already started, and now you're in the middle of the change, which is the act of reading. At some point, you will stop. If you don't finish the book, the cycle remains open. If you do get to the end, the cycle is now closed. Think about if you are reading 10 or 20 books at a time – you'll be under a lot of stress because you simply can't keep up with where things are. Similarly, if you have 10 tasks that you're trying to accomplish and an 11th gets added in, that 11th task may not be stressful in itself; however, it can push you over the edge in regards to your ability to handle so many open cycles at once. This is why we experience stress, not simply in everyday life, but as entrepreneurs who often have so much to handle at any given time.

Think back to our conversation on load and power. Every task is a load, and every load has the potential to become an open cycle. Some loads are not currently open cycles because they are not currently open. Think about it this way: load is the *potential* and the open cycle is the *actual.* When your open cycles or loads are currently open, the more of them that you have, the more stress you are likely to feel.

Some people are able to handle more open cycles than others, but here's the reality: the more open cycles you have in your life, the more stress you will experience. Imagine for a moment that this book you're holding has a reasonable amount of pages. Let's pretend you're also holding *War and Peace*, which is over 1,200 pages long. Think about the difference between those two books – a thin, much easier to digest book versus an extremely thick book.

Now, imagine that every single open cycle in your life is written on a single piece of paper and that all of those pages were bound together like a book. No matter how big the task is or how "stressful" that task may be in and by itself, each open cycle is written on a single page of this imaginary book. Responding to your spouse's text, your business partner's request for a meeting, scheduling a vendor luncheon that you committed to, dealing with a major financial problem – all of these things are single pages in your book. How thick is your book? If every single open cycle in your life – every task, every text, every email, every project, everything that you have to do – is on a single page, how thick is your book? The thicker your book, the more stress you feel. Period. That's how open cycles affect you. You'll want to make sure that you keep your book as thin as possible. You want *this* book – not *War and Peace* – to deal with and manage every day.

When you understand how these open cycles affect you on a greater scale, you'll then be able to try eliminating them from your life. This way, you can help your employees to do the same. After teaching them about the Laws of Open Cycles and helping them to manage their stress, the business will also become less stressed. This is one of the secrets to being able to exit without exiting, which is why one of my core strategies is eliminating stress. Overall, the best way to do this is to understand the power of managing your open cycles.

CONDUCTING AN OPEN CYCLES INVENTORY

Let me give you something to think about further. This is an actual activity that I take my clients through. It's called an *Open Cycles Inventory.* There are four steps involved with taking this inventory.

Step One

Make a list of every open cycle in your life. This activity should take you about three to four hours the first time you do it. I recommend doing this on a piece of paper or a whiteboard, but not in a digital format. Don't do it on a computer, a tablet, or your phone because you won't be able to step back from it and view everything all at once. It's necessary to physically connect with your pen while writing everything down. Be thoughtful with your list and think through everything.

For example, some open cycles for me currently are that I probably have 10 email messages that I need to respond to. I have a letter of intent on a business purchase that I need to complete. I also have to plan dinner with some friends this weekend. I have a motorcycle trip coming up in about three weeks that I need to prepare for. From a business standpoint, I need to rework some scheduling issues with my coaching clients. I have new coaching clients that signed up this week, and I need to have my assistant send agreements to them. These are just a few of the open cycles I have going on right at this very moment.

Ideally, you list every single open cycle in your life – business and personal – but if you just want to limit it to business right now, that's fine too. Again, think very carefully about anything that might be an open cycle for you. Don't leave anything out. One pro tip is to get your business partner, assistant, or your business coach to help you with this activity the first time you do it. They will remember open cycles that you need to write down that may have slipped your mind. Inevitably there are open cycles that you forgot about but have been causing stress in your subconscious. Whether or not you remember them has no bearing on how they affect your stress levels. Every task – no matter how small, no matter how big, and no matter if you remember it at all – still affects your stress level.

Step Two

Divide your list into three sections. Section one consists of cycles that you can close today. Section two includes cycles that you can close with a little planning and forethought and you should be able to close within 2 to 3 weeks at most. Section three is made up of cycles that will take a lot of effort and maybe even help from outside forces to close.

How would you divide this into these three sections? Do the Open Cycles Inventory on a whiteboard and use a black marker to list these things, and then take a blue marker and go back to place an asterisk or underline all of the tasks that are in section one, which are cycles you can close today. For example, answering text messages and emails should be cycles you can close today. Maybe there's a phone call you need to make to someone, or a report that you can turn in tomorrow. These are all cycles that can be wrapped up today. Mark those with your blue marker.

Then, do the same thing with your section two cycles but use a different color marker. Go through and mark the cycles that you can close with a little planning and forethought. If you can't close it today or tomorrow, but with a little planning you can have it closed within the next 2-3 weeks, those are open cycles that get marked in the second section of your list.

Finally, do the same for the third section with a different color marker than the first two. These are the cycles that take a lot of effort or maybe even help from outside forces. For example, if you're working on refinancing your office building, there's only so much you can do at any specific time to get that done. The open cycle may be refinancing the real estate, but then you break down the open cycles into smaller pieces and say, *"Okay, I have to send tax returns to my banker. I need to sign a disclosure agreement, or schedule an appraisal."* These are things you can do, but some you're not able to do alone. You have to wait until they give you approval, or you have to wait until the appraisal comes back. This third section of your Open Cycles Inventory will be made up of things that you're waiting on other people to do, or things that are going to take a long time for you to accomplish. These are your section three open cycles.

Step Three

Now that your list is completed and you've divided it into three sections, begin closing the first and second sections of open cycles as soon as possible! You will be amazed at how much better you will feel as you start closing open cycles. This is how we know the law is true. Your stress levels will begin dropping at a noticeable rate as soon as you begin closing these open cycles from the first and second sections of your inventory.

Let me give you an example of how this worked for someone I know. I once shared this with a mastermind group that I was involved in. The guys in the group were blown away by this and leaned in deeply to the concept. One of them came to me after the presentation and confided in me that his wife – who was a very successful business owner – had been dealing with panic attacks for a long time. They had become overwhelming for her, and he was worried that doing this exercise would induce another panic attack. Of course, I told him I'm no psychologist and cannot speak to how this will actually play out in real life for her and her panic attacks, but I was reasonably confident that this would help her. *"While she might initially feel a sense of panic and stress as she starts the inventory, she will likely feel an immediate sense of relief once she starts working though closing the open cycles in the first section of the inventory,"* I suggested. Weeks later, he came to me and said that his wife responded to the Open Cycles Inventory just as I had predicted. Through this process, her stress levels decreased dramatically almost immediately.

Step Four

Next, work through the third section with as much effort as possible but without opening new open cycles along the way that are related to these. This is going to take more time and planning than the other two sections of your list. Just stay the course and commit to closing them as soon as possible.

As you work through this part of your inventory, you must realize that there are a lot of things you may have assumed at one point that are now not true. You may need to "eat crow" and apologize to others. You might have bitten off more than you can chew. It's time to deal with these realities. Where possible, let people know that you overcommitted and that you need to back out of things you simply cannot handle. While uncomfortable for the moment, closing those open cycles will start to melt the stress away even faster than when you started working through the first section of your inventory.

Of course, the things in this section that are still active and true must be dealt with. But because they are big tasks, you will be tempted to open other cycles to deal with these bigger tasks, or you will try to ignore them altogether. Procrastination is actually just prolonging the open cycle and adding to your stress levels. Don't do that. Just break the tasks down into smaller, more manageable bite-sized pieces and attack them one step at a time. When you do this, you will begin to feel the stress levels drop.

PRO TIPS FOR MANAGING OPEN CYCLES

Tip #1: Successful people evaluate their open cycles on a regular basis. Be sure to schedule an Open Cycle Inventory at least once a month, although I recommend doing this at least once a week. The first time will take you three to four hours, but if you start doing it more often – every week to two weeks, or even once a month – it's going to become only a 30-minute process. When you do this consistently, you will keep managing your open cycles and managing your stress.

Tip #2: Don't open cycles in your life unnecessarily. If someone tries to open one for you, or if you see that you're about to open a new cycle that could cause you to feel overwhelmed, you must learn to recognize that. Instead, say this: *"I don't have time to open that cycle right now. I'm going to delay that."* Then, write it on a piece of paper, stick it somewhere, and go back to it later. If you allow your brain to open that cycle, in the same way that you ask your computer to open another tab, your computer eventually won't be able to keep up. In the same way, your brain also can't keep up. Make sure that you're managing your open cycles appropriately, as they're so important for your overall stress levels to remain at bay.

In the book *The Seven Habits of Highly Effective People* by Steven Covey, he talks about a concept called "Shrink Your Circle of Concern." This basically states that you need to make sure you don't allow yourself to get concerned with things that are not within your purview or not within your ability to handle. That's what open cycles are in a nutshell. Sometimes open cycles don't need to exist in your life, and you've opened them anyway. Unfortunately, this causes you more stress. In fact, the stress that you're feeling is not because of any particular event or task in your life, but instead because you have too many open cycles.

Tip #3: Give yourself permission to temporarily close open cycles that cannot be closed immediately so that you can reduce load and increase power. This is how you allow yourself to gain a greater margin, as we discussed in the last chapter. For example, if you find on your Open Cycles Inventory that you have a cycle you can't close because you can't deal with it right now, although it's becoming a major problem – maybe a tax issue or a financing situation – you need to give yourself temporary permission to close that and come back to it later. Allowing yourself to do this is critical to reducing stress. If you let these kinds of issues eat away at you, it will increase your load and decrease your power. All of this will not only cause stress in the moment but also compound stress.

DON'T TRY TO MANAGE TIME – MANAGE YOUR FOCUS

Before we conclude this chapter on eliminating stress – the second core principle that will lead you to the exit lifestyle – I want to give you another tactical exercise to help you do this. One of the fallacies that was taught by modern YouTube and Instagram gurus is that time management is important. The reality is that **time management is a farce.** Time is a set quantity that cannot be changed or managed any more than you can transform the flow of a river with your hands. "Managing" time is not possible.

What we *can* manage is our focus. How we focus our own time is completely within our control. One of the things I teach my clients in my coaching program and in my courses is how to use a tool that I created called the *10 Block Weekly Scheduling Method.* It's a way to manage your focus, time, and open cycles. I'm going to give you an explanation of how this works in real life and how you can begin using it. James used this to his advantage from day one when he started his business. It's one of the reasons why he was not stressed out as he grew and scaled his business.

Unlike James, Edward bought into the lie about time management. Edward was a voracious reader and read many books on time management. It seemed to him like a new time management book was released every month. He followed all the gurus' teachings about managing time: organizing, goal-setting, communication, planning, prioritizing, etc. He did it all. What he never was able to figure out was how to get *more* time, which is what the gurus seemed to promise. It seemed to him that every book promised more time, yet it never materialized. In his pursuit of more time, he only became more stressed.

The reason time never materialized for Edward is because it simply can't. Period. Time cannot be changed, altered, or forced to expand. You, like me and every other person on the planet, only get 168 hours per week. That's it. No matter how you try to wrangle more time out of your week, you cannot do it. But, like I said, you can manage how you use that time. The only way to do this is by managing what you *focus* on.

James, on the other hand, was aware of how the brain functions and used it to his advantage so that he could manage his focus and grow a business that didn't require so many of his 168 hours per week. There is a part of the brain called the reticular activating system (RAS). The RAS is one of the most important aspects because its function relates specifically to how focus management works. It filters and prioritizes sensory information to let the mind remain focused and alert. Someone once declared that the RAS acts like the ignition system of the brain. It awakens you from the humdrum, monotonous patterns of your day, and into a state of heightened awareness. Modern time management gurus mostly ignore the RAS as it relates to how we truly function.

Remember when you bought your car? It is likely that before you bought that specific car, you rarely noticed them on the highway. Now that you own one, you see them everywhere. Why? Because your RAS is now aware of something that you are focused on and allows you to see those cars everywhere. Previously, your RAS filtered them out because it assumed they weren't important. Your RAS determines what is important based on what you focus on. If that's negative thoughts, your RAS will start feeding you more negative thoughts and will remind you of negative emotions. It will even allow you to start seeing the negative side of things in the world around you, because it thinks that is what you want. It doesn't know any better. Focus on positive thoughts and your subconscious will begin filtering out negative thoughts. Then, your RAS will make you aware of all the good things that are going on around you.

If you want to take full advantage of your 168 hours each week, you must give your RAS reasons to feed you the information that will make you most efficient and most likely to get stuff done. How do you do that? One way is by blocking your schedule out each week so that you force yourself to focus only on tasks you deem important during those blocks of time. What you will find when you do this is that your RAS will start feeding you information, creative ideas, and energy during those blocks of time to help you complete those tasks more effectively and efficiently than ever before. Jumping from one task to another all the time is counterproductive and actually steals time from you.

Allow me to give you a quick exercise to do on your own that will illustrate how focus works. Take out a blank piece of paper, a pen, and your phone with a stopwatch app. You're going to time yourself while you write some things down. Do this twice and then compare your times to see the difference.

First, time yourself writing the entire alphabet in one column (A-Z). Once you write all of the letters in the first column, create a second column next to the letters with numbers 1-26. It will look like this:

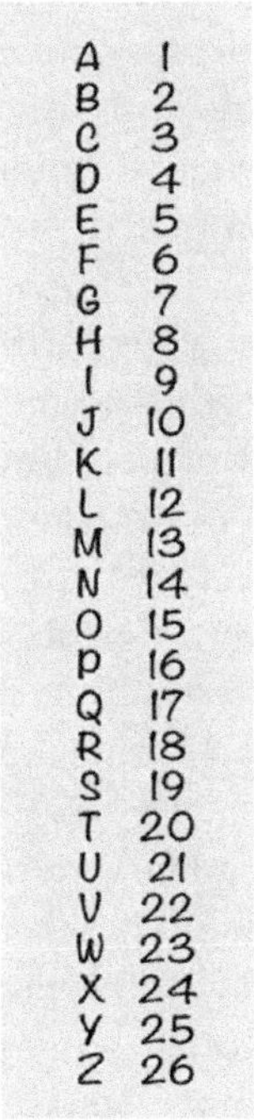

Image 2.1

Go ahead and do the first part of the exercise and time yourself. At the bottom of the page, write your time.

Now, on a different part of that same piece of paper, do this again but with one slight difference. This time, go one *row* at a time rather than one *column* at a time. For example, you will write the letter A and next to it the number 1. Then, you will go to the next row and write the letter B under letter A and then write the number 2 under number 1 and so forth. You'll do this A 1…B 2…C 3 pattern until you finish with Z 26. Time yourself again, and then write down the time at the bottom of the page.

Most people will be able to do the first part of the exercise in 35-39 seconds. For the second part of the exercise, most will take an additional 10-12 seconds to complete it. Why does it take longer to write the same data on a piece of paper simply by alternating between letters and numbers? It's because of focus – or a lack of focus. Contrary to popular belief, multitasking is not efficient. Our brains are not designed to multitask. In fact, we actually work slower when we multitask, which is illustrated by the exercise you just completed.

Let me give you some supporting data on why you shouldn't be jumping back and forth, and instead should keep your focus. I want you to make an estimate of how many times you're distracted on an average workday. Now, take that number and multiply it by 25. That's how many minutes of concentration that you're losing each day. It takes an average of about 25 minutes to return to the original task after an interruption, according to Gloria Mark, who studies digital distraction at the University of California, Irvine.

In another study by a Harvard professor, the average person is distracted or interrupted every 40 seconds when working in front of their computer. Employees spend more than 90 minutes every day – that's seven and a half hours every week – recovering from email interruptions. What I am about to teach you with this 10-Block Weekly Schedule method is the key to eliminating stress by keeping you (and your RAS) focused on what you should be doing on a regular basis, not what's urgent at the moment. Again, this is the tool that James used to his advantage while scaling his company.

HOW TO CREATE YOUR 10-BLOCK WEEKLY SCHEDULE

Step One – List all of your regularly occurring tasks.

The first step in creating your 10-Block Weekly Schedule, which is all about focus management, is to list all of your regularly occurring tasks. We've already done this in two ways. First, you created a "Load List" in the last chapter – that is, everything that you have to do at any given time because you are an entrepreneur and the owner of a specific business. The second thing I had you do was to create your "Open Cycles" list, which refers to loads that are currently open and need to be addressed.

With this 10 Block Weekly Scheduling Method, I want you to use these lists to help with the first step, which is to write out all of your regularly occurring tasks. In other words, this refers to your monthly meetings with your employees, a weekly meeting with your admin team, a finance meeting every single week, a few hours of marketing work or marketing calls, or a meet-up with vendors once a week. Whatever your ongoing tasks happen to be, the first step in creating a 10 Block Weekly Scheduling Method is to make a list of all of them.

Don't worry about categorizing them by time frame – that is, don't worry if this is a daily, weekly, or monthly item. Simply list whatever is regularly occurring in your schedule. Some of my tasks right now are working out three to four times a week, coaching sessions with my clients every Thursday, writing this book, having a coffee meet-up with a friend on Tuesday mornings, a chiropractor appointment that I go to once a week, writing my newsletter, shooting videos for social media, and more. I also have two other businesses that require me to have meetings with vendors once a week. These are all regularly occurring tasks that I would list. You need to do the same thing.

Step Two – Draw out 10 blocks that represent the morning and afternoon of the five days of your workweek.

The second step in creating your 10-Block Weekly Schedule is to draw out 10 blocks each representing the morning or afternoon of the five days of your work week. Most of us work Monday through Friday. What you will have is a block for Monday morning, a block for Monday afternoon, a block for Tuesday morning, a block for Tuesday afternoon, and so on. This is where the method gets its name: *10-Block Weekly Schedule.*

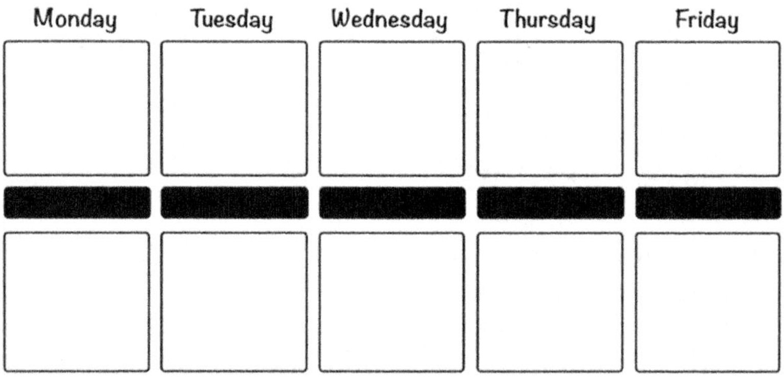

Image 3.1

As a side note, I have had a long-term goal to transition my business to a 4-day workweek, taking Fridays off. In 2022, I made it a goal to begin this in January 2023. So, while the exercise and illustrations I'm going to share with you of my 10-block weekly schedule show five work days, I'm in the middle of transitioning from a 5-day workweek to a 4-day workweek. That means when I update my 10-block weekly schedule for 2023, I will have an 8-block weekly schedule. I'll share more about this later.

With that being said, make your schedule according to when you actually work. If you work Tuesday through Sunday, do

Tuesday through Sunday. The days don't matter–it's the number of blocks that matter. You need to have a block for each portion of the day that you work each week. I recommend using five post-it notes to do this. As a matter of fact, right now on the computer screen where I'm working, I have five post-it notes that say: Monday, Tuesday, Wednesday, Thursday, Friday. They are each divided in half. The top half of each note is the morning, and the bottom half is the afternoon. I can–at a glance–see my 10-Block Weekly Schedule and know what I'm supposed to be focused on at any given time of the day. This has been a huge help to keep me focused. You can do this with anything you'd like, whether it's a whiteboard, a piece of paper, or even Excel. The purpose is that you want to get those 10 blocks drawn out.

The top row of blocks are mornings and the bottom row of blocks are afternoons. Generally speaking, the top blocks are 8:00 – 12:00 and the bottom blocks are 1:00 – 5:00. The black bars between the blocks will be explained later.

Step Three – Assign your weekly tasks to a block.

Now that you have a list of your regularly occurring tasks and your ten blocks drawn out, you can now begin assigning your weekly tasks to a block. You can have more than one task in each block, but try to group them into categories so that you're not switching focus during any one block. For instance, if you have a sales block where you have to do outbound sales calls, you don't want to also put administrative tasks in that same block, because going back and forth between sales tasks and administrative tasks will make you perform worse at both of those tasks. You need to make sure that you're paying attention and focusing. That's why this is a *focus* management tool, not a time management tool.

PRO TIP #1: If you are like most people, there are going to be a few tasks on your weekly list that you have no control over. So, before you assign all of your tasks to blocks, make sure you first write in any tasks or meetings that happen on a regular basis that you do not control. For example, if you have a monthly meeting with shareholders on Tuesday afternoons and it is not a meeting you can move to another block, then write that meeting in the Tuesday afternoon block before you begin assigning other tasks. This way you won't find yourself having to rearrange tasks later to maintain focus on that Tuesday afternoon block.

PRO TIP #2: What time of the day are you most productive? What tasks are the highest and best use of your time? Make sure that those tasks are in the right block. For example, if you are most productive in the mornings and your highest and best use of time is strategic thinking and planning, then make sure you write "Strategic Thinking and Planning" into a morning block before you fill up the space with other, less important tasks.

PRO TIP #3: Pick two to four blocks per week that you label DND ("Do Not Disturb"). In other words, these are blocks for the times when you turn off your email and phone. These are your specific focus times. You want to make sure that you have at least two (though preferably four) blocks of time to do this within your week where you're not going to be disturbed by outside forces. No digital dings, bings, bumps, buzzes, or anything else. It's important that you're not interrupted.

Make sure you are strategic in choosing the tasks that you assign to each block. For example, sales prospecting should be done in the morning blocks, if at all possible. Studies show that sales activities and sales receptiveness is always best in the mornings, not in the afternoons. If you want to get even more specific, Tuesday, Wednesday, and Thursday are your better mornings to do outbound prospecting. On Monday, everyone's trying to get ready for the week. On Friday, everyone's trying to finish work for the weekend. Therefore, Tuesday, Wednesday, and Thursday mornings are going to be your best days for this task.

See illustration below for a sample of what one of my 10-block Weekly Schedules looks like. As you will read below, I recommend changing and updating your 10-block Weekly Schedule at least once a quarter. The one I'm sharing with you here is from mid-2022.

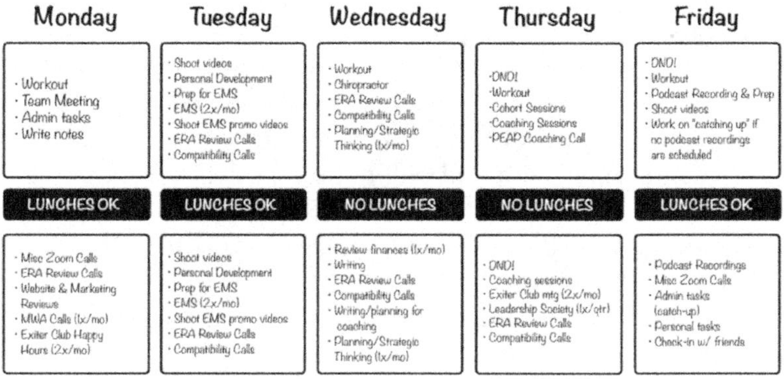

Image 3.2

As you can see in this illustration, I have very clearly organized my weekly tasks into specific blocks of time. Each block has similar activities so that my brain doesn't have to switch from one activity to a totally different activity during the same block. This keeps me efficient and productive. The black bars are for lunch. I only allow people to schedule lunch meetings with me on Mondays, Tuesdays, and Fridays. Those are days that my focus won't be negatively affected by leaving the office to have lunch with someone. I do not leave the office for lunch on days when I need to stay focused. I still eat on those "NO LUNCH" days, but I eat at the office.

Let's review your three steps. First, list all of the regularly occurring tasks. Secondly, draw out 10 blocks that represent your morning and afternoon of your five workdays. And third, start assigning your weekly tasks to blocks. Remember, you can have multiple tasks in a block, and you can have the same task in multiple blocks throughout the week.

BONUS TIPS FOR CRAFTING YOUR 10-BLOCKS WEEKLY SCHEDULE

The first bonus tip is to place your post-it notes (if you're using post-it notes) at the bottom of your computer screen or somewhere on your desk where you can reference them throughout the day. I do this so that I can go into the upper left-hand drawer of my desk and pull out old post-it notes from my previous 10-block schedules, which I have saved for a few years. These are reference points for me to see how things have changed.

Your 10-Block Weekly Schedule will change from time to time, depending upon what season you're in. You need to be prepared to evolve your 10-Block Weekly Schedule as often as it's required, but probably no more than every two-three months. If you do it more than that, you're just confusing yourself and causing open cycles that don't need to be open.

The second bonus tip is to use your Google or Outlook calendar to keep the blocks organized, and share that with your assistant or other team members so they know what's going on. For example, I use Google calendar to create a schedule called "Jason's 10-Block Weekly Schedule." I can go in and block out 8:00 AM to 12:00 PM on Mondays and type in bullet points in the notes of what I'm supposed to be focused on during that block. Then, I can mark myself "free, not busy" so this setup doesn't affect other people's ability to schedule meetings with me. This calendar is only a reference for me and my assistant and not anything that is public-facing. If you allow this digital calendar to mark you as *busy,* then you're eliminating any ability for someone else to book a meeting with you. Your main goal with this calendar is to allow your assistant or other designated people to see what you're doing and also be reminded of what you're supposed to be doing during that time. Then, do that for every block throughout the week. As you get used to doing this, you will be able to pull up your calendar wherever you are and say: *"That's right. This is when I'm supposed to do that task!"*

Let me give you an example. I had a call the other day with someone who reached out to me about wanting to help with marketing on my podcast, *The Root of All Success*. What he told me was actually intriguing, and I really did want to talk to him. I wrote him back and said: *"I do all my marketing stuff on Monday afternoons. So are you available Monday afternoon between 2:00 and 3:00?"* And he said: *"No, I'm not available until Tuesday next week."* I said: *"Okay, then let's talk next Monday when you are available. We can get something scheduled for a Monday afternoon when you are free."*

I didn't let him dictate when I would meet to talk about marketing, because my block is very specific. I only do the marketing stuff on Mondays, so I didn't let him push me into a day when that wasn't going to align with my schedule. This is the same for all of my other blocks. For instance, I record video content for my YouTube channel, Instagram, and LinkedIn twice a week, and I only do that on Tuesdays and Fridays. I make sure to keep my blocks on point so that I allow time each week for these important tasks, while also not straying away from my calendar. This allows me to maintain focus so that I'm not flipping back and forth.

Overall, the 10-Block Weekly Scheduling method will keep you focused on your tasks and make sure that you're looking at what's most important. It will allow you to manage your open cycles and your load with higher productivity and lower stress. If you follow it, you will feel less stressed because you will be able to understand when to do certain tasks. You won't feel like things are always left undone.

If you need help with this, reach out to me. I show my clients how to create their own 10-Block Weekly Schedules and how to implement them into their lives successfully as a part of my 10-Hour Entrepreneur course. Most of my clients find that it takes about six weeks of working with this method before they get fully comfortable with it. At that point, you can start tweaking it every couple of months thereafter. One client I worked with was always very busy and was regularly putting in 60 to 70 hour workweeks. After we worked on designing his 10-Block Weekly Schedule, he had two full blocks with no activities in it, yet every single activity on his weekly schedule was assigned comfortably into a specific block. This showed him that he was not being productive with his time. He found a full 8 hours in his week simply by focusing his tasks into certain blocks. Imagine how much time you will find when you start using this method.

Finally, make sure that you understand this truth: **you cannot manage your time but you can manage your focus**. Therefore, if you manage your focus, your time will be used more efficiently, you will be much more productive, and your stress levels will be reduced to zero. Where your focus goes, energy flows. You can energize your life and the lives of your employees by practicing these methods.

CONCLUSION

Stress is a killer, both literally and figuratively. James and his business were not afflicted with stress – he had totally eliminated it not only from his own life, but from his employees' lives as well. And by extension, this stress-free attitude and way of doing business made James' business run more smoothly, efficiently, and profitably. As you know, businesses that are easy to do business with get more business. Stress-free businesses are easy to do business with. James reaped a huge reward from these stress-free tactics. When he was ready to exit the daily operations, he knew his employees would handle things well and wouldn't allow stress to affect the way they made decisions. Ultimately, this allowed him to step away from the day-to-day without fear of things not getting accomplished.

The second core principle in figuring out how to exit without exiting so that you can live the exit lifestyle is to "Eliminate Stress." I chose that phrase on purpose as opposed to simply *reducing* or *managing* stress. The Law of Open Cycles is very clear about the true cause of stress. Once you understand that law, you can begin leveraging it to your benefit. Understand that your goal should not be to reduce stress or manage it, but to eliminate it. One of the greatest compliments an employee ever gave me was that I was the most "laid back but driven person" she ever met. I am not a stressed person, but that doesn't mean I'm not a hard-charging, high-achiever. I am driven to succeed at very high levels, but I do not use the need for achievement as an excuse to allow myself to be stressed out. One of the blessings of being an entrepreneur is the freedom to choose my destiny. I choose a stress-free life – one that I control based on how I manage my open cycles and how I manage my focus. I won't allow open cycles or calendar events to rule me and cause stress. You don't have to do that either. Go back and re-read this chapter as often as necessary to practice these stress-elimination strategies so that you can have a business that is growing and scaling without stress. Before you know it, you will see yourself less and less stressed out and your business will be growing without your daily oversight.

8. ESTABLISH SYSTEMS AND PROCESSES

Cheryl was a true workaholic. It is one of the regrets she felt as she sat at the closing table, ready to receive a check that would change her life. She knew that all of those hours she put it at the office stole time from her kids that she would never get back. There was also a sense of dread that began to bubble up in her over the realization that after today, she wouldn't have any excuse to work 80-hour weeks. After all, the business would belong to someone else. When the transition period was over, she would have to find something else to occupy her time. Her mistakes were valid, but she was not content to focus on regret during this major milestone in her life. So, she began pondering all of the things she was proud of accomplishing.

One thing that came to mind was how good she had been at systems and processes. As a matter of fact, the buyers were willing to pay top dollar in part due to the fact that her business ran so smoothly. It seemed as if no matter which employee was involved in a task, it always ran the same way and produced predictable results each time. This was something Cheryl had put a ton of effort into over the years. Even though she had regrets about working too much, she was proud of the systems and processes she had built, which made her business tremendously more valuable.

The first major shift in the manufacturing industry came in an era that we now refer to as the Industrial Revolution. The Industrial Revolution was when manufacturing shifted from products being made by hand, to systems and processes that allowed for products to be made in an assembly line. Machines and people performed the same processes inside of a larger system in order to produce a product and an outcome that would be predictable for that organization.

Looking back in history, before the Industrial Revolution started, systems and processes weren't put to use on a mass scale. Instead, each worker had to do the best he or she could. A shoemaker, for example, would make shoes all by himself – the cutting of the leather, the sizing of the pieces, the making of the sole, the stitching of the seams, etc. While the output each time would be similar, there were unique differences in each shoe. The Industrial Revolution taught us that if you implement systems and processes on a large scale, more can be accomplished, profits can be larger for the owners of the company, and the product output can be more predictable, uniform, and of higher quality.

The assembly line was perfected by Henry Ford of Ford Motor Company back in the early 1900's. Ford understood that if a system and a process were aligned together, there would be a predictable outcome with better quality materials, products, and higher profitability. Ford knew that ultimately, with effective and efficient systems and processes in place, everyone wins. His cars would be higher quality, cheaper to manufacture, and more affordable for the customer, only making his company overall become more profitable. The same thing is true today in your own business endeavors as an entrepreneur, which leads us to our third core strategy in the exit without exiting plan: "Establish Systems and Processes."

THE DIFFERENCE BETWEEN SYSTEMS AND PROCESSES

Let's start by talking about the difference between systems and processes. A *process* is a series of steps and decisions involved in the way work is completed, and when adhered to consistently, it can lead to predictable results. A *system* is a group of processes that work together to get work done in the same way every time, which leads to consistency and efficiency and less stress. Systems and processes will allow you to exit the daily operations of your business. Remember, you cannot be the hero forever. At the beginning, yes, but not forever. It's simply not sustainable. One of the ways you can ditch the hero's cape is to establish specific systems and processes that don't rely on you as the central figure to get everything done.

There are dozens of options that can be efficient for every type of business, such as service businesses, product businesses, manufacturing businesses, and digital/technological businesses. Each of those is going to have a need for different types of systems and processes. My recommendation is for you to hire a consultant or a business coach who is well-versed in understanding how systems and processes work. This systems expert will help you identify which systems and processes are most important, how to firm up those that are currently in place, and how to implement those that need to be there so that the business runs like a well-oiled machine. Since this book is general and is not designed to be specific for a particular type of industry, I'm going to focus on the most important system and process for any business – *the sales system.*

There are three parts to the sales system that are made up of multiple processes and are not intended to replace your current sales process. It's important to emphasize that I'm not necessarily asking you to change the way that you do things; instead, look at how what you're doing now fits with this particular system and make adjustments as necessary. In other words, I'm going to teach you how the scaffolding around your particular sales systems and processes should be built. I have outlined three very specific things that if implemented into your sales system, will help you close more deals and generate more revenue. As an example, a recent client I've been coaching saw their revenue increase by 43% in one year after implementing this sales system. It can do the same for you.

PART 1: KNOW THE FOUR REASONS WHY PEOPLE BUY

The first part of this three-part sales system is understanding why people buy. People only do what they're motivated to do, and you simply cannot motivate them to do otherwise. You can only tap into their motivating factors. This particular part of the sales system is going to help you with prospecting and understanding what motivates potential clients.

Every business leader, every entrepreneur, and every salesperson struggles with prospecting. It's one of the most important parts of your business, because if you don't have prospects to talk to, you can never pitch. If you don't pitch, you can't sell. If you can't sell, you don't have any money. Everything starts with prospecting.

The problem with most prospecting is that salespeople end up pursuing deals with potential prospects or potential customers who are never likely to buy in the first place. This type of sales behavior always reminds me of Jim Carey's character, Lloyd, in the 1994 movie *Dumb and Dumber.* Lloyd is talking to Mary, the woman he has a huge crush on. He asks her what the chances are of the two of them getting together. While Lloyd is totally smitten with Mary, she has no interest in him. She politely tells him the chances of her going out with him are "one in a million." In response, Llyod smiles optimistically and says, "So you're telling me there's a chance!"

Every salesperson thinks that there's a chance with every person they talk to – they're eternally optimistic, just like Lloyd.

Sales - lose early

While part of that is good, the other part can lead to lots of wasted time. I often turn to one of my mentors, Bud Suse, about this topic. He's the author of *Closing the Whales: The Anatomy of Major Deals, A Proven Process for Complex, High Tech Sales Campaigns.* His second book is *Winning Complex Enterprise Sales: A True Story of the Best Campaign Ever for Sales Teams, Civic and Political Leaders; Consensus Generation at its Best*, which I wrote the foreword to. I highly recommend both books. Bud taught me a long time ago that if you're going to be good at sales, you've got to lose early. After all, you don't want to spend weeks, months, or perhaps even years in a sales cycle with a potential customer only to find out that you came in second. You want to lose early. And if you can tell that you're going to lose early, you can walk away and spend more time on deals that are likely to close. This is a key point to understand.

You're not going to win every deal every time, so be ready to lose early if you can. Every salesperson knows what a *yes* sounds like, but few know what a *no* sounds like. No salesperson will ever win 100% of the opportunities they pursue. We're all going to lose sales. And the successful salesperson will remember the motto of great losers: lose early. You must be very selective when choosing which opportunities to pursue. It costs a lot of time and money to engage with a potential customer. If they eventually do not buy from you, you've spent possibly thousands of dollars for no return. That's a bad investment. Instead, learn to be an early loser.

To be an early loser, you have to be a winning prospector, which means you need to understand the reasons why people buy. I suggest that your CRM system should be set up so that when your sales people log in the information on why a deal was lost, they can only choose one of four reasons because there are only four reasons why anyone buys anything – ever. In order to be successful as a salesperson, you need to understand how each of these four reasons play into your prospect's buying decision. At least one of these four motivating factors must be present. The more that are present, the more likely the sale will happen. Let's look at the four reasons, which are: *relationship, need, timing,* and *money.*

RELATIONSHIP

A good relationship is critical to buying. I define this reason as "the motivating factor in a sale when the prospect has **goodwill and trust** in the product, service, salesperson, or company." You know that a good relationship is present when the prospect likes you, when he trusts you, when he listens to you, and when he serves you. Let me break that down.

There is a principle in the Bible called "the person of peace principle" from the book of Luke. The story is told of a time when Jesus is sending out the disciples to spread the Gospel into different towns. He tells them to go to each house and say, *"Peace be with you."* If the peace is returned to them, then they're to stay in that house and share the Gospel with them, because the peace returning to them means that the people in the home are willing to listen. They are demonstrating trust and goodwill in the disciples by letting them stay in their home and by feeding them. It's only then, after the peace has been returned, that they can actually share the Gospel.

Obviously, this situation wasn't about sales, but the same principle applies to what we do in sales. If you can find prospects who like you, who trust you, who listen to you, and who serve you, then you know that there's a relationship present. In sales parlance, what we're talking about is that you've got to have a prospect who at least likes you. Now, that doesn't mean you're best friends, but the person at least has to like you. If they do, then they can have trust in you, be willing to listen to you, and can serve you.

What does it mean for a prospect to serve you? Well, they're certainly not going to invite you to their home, let you stay there, and feed you while you try to pitch them. But what it does mean is that if you're trying to set appointments, send information, ask for data back from them, continually discussing, or setting meetings – that's all a form of service. They're serving you through the process of you selling to them and them being responsive, which is important. If they're not showing responsiveness, you can be sure that they don't like you, they probably are not going to listen to you, and they do not trust you. People tend to buy from people they like – it's plain and simple. The relationship that a prospect has with the seller will sometimes outweigh all other logical reasons to buy. If that relationship is clearly not present, it's a good time to lose early.

NEED

While relationships are a factor in closing many sales, they aren't the only one. Need is another motivating factor in closing deals. It's motivating because it has to do with the prospect's **perceived value** in the product or service offered. If the value of the product or service outweighs the prospect's current situation without it, then a need – whether perceived or actual – is established. This becomes the motivating factor in sales that have to do with that perceived value.

Perceived value in the product or service offered is what must be present for need to occur. In other words, if the prospect believes that he or she can live without your product or service, then there's no need. Although true, people sometimes buy things simply because they want to. They don't really need the item, in terms of the dictionary definition of *need*, but they want it. It was the great Zig Ziglar who said, *"Nobody is going to pay $100 for something they perceive as worth only $10."* This statement is very true. You're typically not going to pay $100 for something that you think is worth $10. As an entrepreneur, your sales system from the start has to work diligently to establish a perceived need within the product. In other words, if you can imagine for a moment that the prospect's life is at a certain level or their business is at a certain level, and you're offering something that would increase that level, then you've created a need for your product. That's what you want, and that's what motivates buying behavior and closes deals.

A good salesperson will have a sense of his prospect's needs – the actual need and their perceived need. If neither of these needs appear to be present, it's likely a sign that a closing isn't going to happen any time soon.

TIMING

Timing is the motivating factor in sales that has to do with how the prospect's overall need for the product intersects with other factors inside the prospect's business. This is called ***context***, which is the key word here. For instance, the context of a sale might have a lot to do with things that aren't directly discussed in your sales process, such as fiscal year, budget constraints, and other competing objectives for the business or for the individual. All of these things affect timing.

This is a huge buying factor that many salespeople simply don't pay attention to, and it's the one that you have the least control over. Generally speaking timing is only a veto decision. In other words, the relationship could be solid, the prospect may need the service, the money may make sense and be affordable. However, timing can trump the entire deal. You have to always pay attention to timing. If the timing isn't right, it's better to get a sense of that earlier rather than later. The earlier you have a feel for the contextual factor of your client's business in relation to the timing of a potential sale, the better. If it doesn't seem to be right, take the opportunity to lose early.

MONEY

Money is the motivating factor in sales that has to do with the prospect's **ability to pay** for the product or service. Do they have the ability to pay? Can they afford it? What financial implications does the sale have on the customer after they make the purchase? "Money" as a motivating factor in sales has nothing to do with the cost; it's about the ability to pay. Cost is addressed in "need," which is about perceived value.

To most people, it seems like money is the easiest factor to consider in any sales process. However, it's not as cut-and-dry as you might think. Sometimes the product or service is affordable and reasonably priced, but the fiscal constraints make buying impossible. Therefore, the sale will be impossible and simply won't happen. Money, as a buying reason, isn't about how much it costs. Instead, it's about budgets, fiscal year issues, borrowing ability, and the ability to pay. That's the key idea here – **ability to pay**. Your prospect might like you, have a need, and the timing is perfect. But if the person can't pay for it, then you're unlikely to close that sale in the near term. This is when you need to be mindful of your own time and resources so you're not making a large investment for a minimal chance of return.

CREATE A DISCOVERY CALL SCRIPT

Let's put all of this together. If you're pitching your product or service to particular prospects, and you want to make sure that these four reasons are present, how do you do that? Your sales system has to include a process by which you ask the right questions very early in the process.

I recommend that you and your sales team work together to create a Discovery Call Script, or sometimes called a Compatibility Call Script. At your first meeting with a potential client, you ask specific questions to help uncover which of the four reasons why they would buy from you are present and which should be addressed. These particular questions have to be centered around these four reasons:

Make sure the relationship is established. (i.e., do they have trust and goodwill in you?)

Make sure that need is established. (i.e., do they perceive value in your offer?)

Make sure that timing is established and understood. (i.e., is the context to buy favorable?)

Make sure that money is established. (i.e., do they have the ability to pay?)

You cannot finish that first meeting without understanding those four things. That is why understanding why people buy is the first step in your sales system.

I've written an e-book called *Why People Buy* that dives into these four reasons in a lot more depth than I'm able to do in this text. You can check it out here: *therealjasonduncan.com/whypeoplebuy*.

CREATE A 20-POINT MATRIX

The second part of the three-step sales system is to establish a method that identifies your ideal prospect as quickly and efficiently as possible. I designed a sales tool called The 20-point Matrix. The idea behind it is that if I eliminate opportunities from my pipeline that I am reasonably sure won't ever close, I will sell more and make more money. This 20-point Matrix will help you identify good opportunities and bad opportunities within five minutes of meeting with a prospect, which can eliminate countless hours of wasted time pursuing avenues that will never close. In addition, your 20-point Matrix will be designed specifically for you and your business.

I originally created this custom 20-point Matrix for one of my companies – the company that I exited several years ago – because I needed to create a system that didn't rely on me. I collaborated with my leadership team to identify the core criteria for good versus bad selling opportunities. We discovered there were certain factors that actually worked in our favor, contrary to what we thought would've been true. At the time, we were doing lighting projects in large buildings across the United States. Our assumption was that if a single customer had multiple locations, that would make it a better deal, or a better project for us than if a customer had a single location. After we ran the numbers, we found out that a single location is actually much better. We make more money, the project goes more smoothly, and the customer ends up liking us more on single-location projects. We discovered multiple factors along these lines.

It is going to be difficult to build your 20-point Matrix based on reading a single chapter in this book. My recommendation would be for you to enroll in my 10-Hour Entrepreneur course, and I will walk you through how to create that matrix in detail. There are six overarching primary criteria that you need to identify to qualify an opportunity. Remember that the number six is really important. I've worked with customers and clients to come up with different numbers: five, six, four, seven, eight, ten. But six has proven to be the ideal number. To create this 20-point Matrix, you're going to first identify the top six criteria for your ideal customer.

3 STEPS TO CREATE YOUR 20-POINT MATRIX

Step 1: Identify the Top Six Criteria of Your Ideal Client – How are you going to figure that out? You have to go look at the data. Just like what we did with my team, we assumed certain things about the data that simply were not true. We thought that working with a senior facility manager, for example, was the best thing for us. In actuality, when we were working with a president, owner, or CFO, we had a better shot. Our assumptions were not always correct. We had to look at the data to discover the reality of this.

What you're going to have to do is look at the data for your business and find what similarities are occurring in projects that you liked, went well, ran smoothly, offered a return, and left the customer happy. Look at those interactions you've had with customers who bought from you, and then you should be able to start identifying what criteria is important to forming a good deal.

For example, in my own business, the six criteria were:
Location (geographical)
Number of locations
Facility size (square footage)
Contact person's title or role
Type of building (e.g., school, hospital, warehouse, etc.)
Bid scenario (e.g., formal bid process, no bid, etc.)

We realized that if we identified those top six criteria in a prospect, we would know with great confidence whether or not this deal was going to work out.

Step 2: Rank the Criteria – Now that you've determined your six criteria, rank the levels of each of the six criteria individually, one to five, based on the sub-criteria. For example, location was one of the criteria for my company, which was based in Nashville, Tennessee. Anything located in the Greater Nashville area gets a five because that's the ideal; the rating becomes successively lower the farther out we move from there.

Let's look at another criteria so that this becomes a little bit clearer. The contact person's role or title was another item I needed to look over. The owner, CEO, and President gets a five because that's the ideal. A CFO or a COO gets a four. A director of facilities gets a three, as does a plant manager. An engineer, a maintenance person, or controller gets two. Any other title in that business only gets one.

Step 3: Calculate the Results – When you look at these six criteria and score each on a one to five scale, you're going to come up with a total possible score of 30. Six criteria times five points is 30, but nobody is ever going to get a 30. The reason I've named this the 20-Point Matrix is because you are looking for 20 points or higher. An ideal customer for you should have 20 points or more. Here's how this is going to work.

Once all six categories are scored and totaled, you're going to get a number between 6–30. The higher the score, the better, obviously. Your scores should guide the decision for you and your team in terms of continuing to pursue this opportunity, or stopping.

Here are some notes to consider:

Generally speaking, opportunities that score 20 or above are good. You should be able to move forward with these without any hesitancy.

If the score is between 15 and 20, I recommend your system have a rule that says the salesperson must talk to the Director of Sales to determine if there's a reason to continue pursuing it. For example, if it was a highly recommended referral or if it's a customer that you're familiar with on another product, but who doesn't really fit the ideal prospect on this one, you may decide to pursue it because you have a good relationship with that prospect. Although, you should get your Sales Manager or Director of Sales involved in that decision. Don't let your salespeople make that decision on their own, because these eternally optimistic individuals are going to pursue deals that are not likely to close, which wastes your time and money. They, like Lloyd in *Dumb and Dumber*, think they have a chance.

Scores that are below 15 are never to be pursued – ever. I don't care if it's your mom! Don't pursue sales opportunities under 15, because they're very likely to be a waste of time, waste of energy, waste of resources, and ultimately not make you any money. The likelihood of that person buying from you to begin with is so low that it doesn't make sense to follow through.

Implementing a 20-Point Matrix into your sales system is extremely important. I've included a sample here. (See image 4.1)

Again, you can take my 10-Hour Entrepreneur course where I will walk you through this entire process in detail.

	LOCATIONS	# OF LOCATIONS	FACILITY SIZE	CONTACT TITLE	TYPE OF BUILDING	BID SCENARIO
5	Greater Nashville Area	1	1,000,000	President/CEO Owner	Hospital/ Warehouse	No Bid
4	2-3 Hours from Nashville	2-3	750k-1m	CFO/COO	School	—
3	4-6 Hours from Nashville	—	250-750k	Facility Manager	Office	Informal Bid
2	—	—	100-250k	Controller	Commercial	—
1	Flight Required	More than 3	Under 100k	Other	Retail/Restaurant	Formal Bid

Image 4.1

THE PERFECT SALES SEQUENCE

The third step is something I call the Perfect Sales Sequence. Just like any other sequence, it needs to go in order. It is not a replacement for your overall process, but it's a sequence by which you should do certain things throughout your sales process.

This is a proven method that's based on research originally produced in a book called *The Challenger Sale,* by Mathew Dixon and Brent Adamson. It is one of the bibles, so to speak, that I use when I teach other people about sales. What they discovered in *The Challenger Sale* was that the people who outperformed other salespeople almost two-to-one followed a certain sequence in their sales process. Over the last decade, I have followed that sequence to a T, but I have also realized that there are certain things about that sequence that they left out. I wanted to make the process easier to remember and follow.

What I've done is take their research, and my real-life experiences, and come up with something I refer to as *The Perfect Sales Sequence*. There are seven pieces to it, and they are all "F" words so that you can remember them easily. Let's look at each of them here.

1. FOUNDATION – Build That All-Important Relationship

The first part of the sequence is building the proper foundation. Just like when you're building a house, you have to first make sure the foundation is solid. Every single sales opportunity must start by building the proper foundation. What does that look like? This happens when you make sure that the prospect recognizes that you understand them. This means showing them that you have done your pre-call research, which can prove to be worth millions of dollars for you.

You should research every potential client, his industry, what their challenges are, and more so that when you show up on that first call or when you meet with them for the first time, you can say: *"Hey, when we meet with people in your industry, what we're finding is they're facing these types of challenges (and list them out). Are you facing similar challenges, or is there something different in your business that you're going through?"* When you say something like that, you are firmly establishing the foundation that you are an expert who understands their issues, and they will be able to begin to trust you. Always keep in mind the first of the four reasons why anybody buys – relationships.

This part of the sequence of foundation building is all about creating the relationship. It's not just walking into their office and noticing that they have a bass hanging on the wall and saying, *"Oh, you like to fish? I like to fish too."* Don't do that. Unless you are an avid fisherman who fishes every waking hour, you're not allowed to mention that bass on the wall. That is disingenuous, people see through it, and it's not helping you. What you're trying to do here is show that you are an expert who understands their issues and challenges, not only in their business, but in their industry as well. You're there to help them. The Perfect Sales Sequence starts with building the proper foundation and establishing this relationship.

2. FRAMING – Set the Parameters of the Conversation

The second part of the Perfect Sales Sequence is framing, or in some instances reframing, the conversation. When you build anything, you start with the foundation and then you begin the framing. You frame up the walls and you frame up the edges. You get everything ready so that you can build around it.

What most salespeople don't understand is that every prospect you meet with has an idea already preconceived in their mind about what you're going to be pitching. For instance, one of my companies is a lighting company. When we met with prospects, almost every single time they would think that all we were going to do is come in and talk about light bulbs. In actuality, we were not talking about light bulbs at all. Light bulbs are just the tool that we used to accomplish the outcome that we were intending to get, which was saving money and saving energy. What I had to do, and what my sales team had to do, was to frame the conversation around the proper outcome. For example, if you're selling real estate, you're not just selling dirt, bricks, and mortar and sticks. What you're selling is a preferred future, the enjoyment of life, the betterment of the business, or the ability to serve customers better once that piece of real estate becomes owned by the prospect.

Remember this! People don't buy WHAT you're selling… they buy the RESULT of what you're selling.

You have to frame – or sometimes reframe—the conversation around what you're actually talking about early on in the process, and then continually point back to what you're really there for. It's not just light bulbs, or whatever it is that you're selling. Again, this helps to build that relationship. You thwart their assumptions, which surprises them and makes them like and even trust you.

3. FIGURES – Talk about the Cost of Inaction

The third part of the Perfect Sales Sequence is all about the figures. More specifically, it's about putting the prospects' potential inaction in figures that they can understand. There is always a cost associated with inaction and not doing something. If I don't upgrade to the new widget that you're selling, there's a cost that I will then incur through my inaction. There's an actual dollar amount attributed to that, and I need to be aware of it as the potential customer. At this point, your job in the Perfect Sales Sequence is to expose that cost of inaction. You must make sure that the prospect understands if they don't act, or if something doesn't change within their business, there is a risk that they'll be exposed to and a cost they're going to incur that they may not yet perceive.

For example, if I'm selling an LED lighting project to a hospital, the cost of inaction is wasted money going to the electric utilities or to the maintenance costs that could have been recovered and spent on hiring more nurses or remodeling the emergency room. There are other ways to spend that wasted money. To conclude, in your sales sequence, you need to expose that very specific cost of inaction in figures that the prospect will clearly understand.

4. FEELINGS – Appeal to the Prospect's Emotions

The fourth step in the Perfect Sales Sequence is to appeal to the prospects' feelings. You want to give them an emotional reason to act. This is the piece of the sale sequence that I'm the worst at doing. I'm not a very emotional person, so I find that this part is harder for me. Nevertheless, I know that every buying decision is made emotionally and then justified logically. Every time you've bought a house, a phone, a car, a mailbox, or a meal, there was an emotional decision made first. Even if that's on the most minimal level. Even if it is just something you wanted or thought your life would be better with. Once you make that emotional commitment, you then attempt to rationalize it with logic.

For example, when you buy a house or decide to rent an apartment, you say to yourself: *"Oh yeah, I can definitely see myself living here. I love this place."* That's emotion. There's an emotional reason to act that arises first, and then you start to look at the money to attempt to justify the purchase logically. *"Okay. Can I afford it? Well, it's an $800,000 house. I can afford it."* If you cannot justify it logically, it will go like this: "*Ok, it's an $8 million house. I can't afford it.*" Your emotions drive the desire, and then logic allows for it to happen or not.

In your sales sequence, you not only have to expose the cost of inaction and talk about all the figures and money, but you also have to discuss the emotional reasons to act. To do so, you have to dig deep. Why would the person *want* to do this? What are their individual business economic drivers? What are the individual value drivers that will help them make this decision from an emotional perspective?

5. FAIRNESS – Time to Secure Agreement on THE Solution

The fifth step in the Perfect Sales Sequence is the customer agreeing to the actual solution to the problem that you've just illustrated throughout the sales process. Someone once said that a sale is nothing more than two people agreeing on the truth. I really like that definition because it's about fairness. The two parties agree that the truth is, the prospect needs the solution you are proposing to solve that problem. That's very fair. Both parties then find a mutually beneficial solution to their needs.

Let me give you a little tip here: The key is *the* solution, not *your* solution. It's really important that you're not pitching *your* solution yet, because *your* solution cannot be purchased until they first purchase *the* solution. Read that again.

I'll give you an example. If you are a shoe salesperson and you go to a group of people who don't wear shoes, they will not care whether or not your shoes are better than every other shoe on the market. You first have to sell them on the idea of *shoes* before you can sell them on *your* shoes. So you must refer to Step 5 of the Perfect Sales Sequence in order to secure an agreement that THE solution to their need is shoes. Then, you can move to step 6 in the process, which is all about YOUR shoes and how they are indeed the most beneficial solution for their needs.

6. FULFILLMENT – Sell Them on YOUR Solution

Step 6 of the Perfect Sales Sequence is getting the prospect to agree that YOUR solution is the one they need. Here is the first time in the entire process where you get to talk about YOUR solution. Finally, you've earned the right to present YOUR solution. If you've done the sequence correctly, they have seen you as an expert who understands their situation, they understand and are concerned about the cost of inaction, they are emotionally bought in, and they agree with you on THE solution to their problem. Now you get to tell them how you are the perfect person with the perfect product or service to provide that solution that they agree will help them.

Let's continue with the shoe example. You have a prospect who agrees that shoes will solve their problem. That's step 5 – they agree on THE Solution. Then you present your product as the best solution, the one that will best fulfill their needs: *"I've got this amazing shoe. This shoe is the best shoe in the world. It does everything that you said you want, and I've got it right here. This shoe meets every need that you have."*

If you've followed the sequence correctly, you will find that the prospect is prepared to buy your solution. At the beginning of the process, they didn't care about your particular solution. They didn't care about you. They only cared about whether or not you understood them and their unique problem. Once you demonstrated that you did care about them and understood their problem, you presented the solution and they agreed it would help. Finally, you've earned the right to tell them about YOUR solution. So go on, tell them how wonderful your solution is, how it miraculously solves every problem you agreed on earlier, and fits the solution they agreed to a moment ago. This is when sales become easy.

7. FORMALIZE – Close the Deal by Asking for the Sale

The seventh step in the Perfect Sales Sequence is to formalize or close the deal. *Ask for the sale!* How many times have you been in a meeting with a salesperson who tried to sell you something, and they never asked for the sale? They went through the whole process and at the end said, *"Well, I guess I'll follow up with you later. Can I check back in in two weeks?"* They didn't ask for the sale. *"Are you ready to do this? Are you ready to sign on the dotted line? Are you ready to buy? Are you ready to make the purchase? Are you ready to make the investment? Are you ready to get started?"* These are types of questions that need to be asked to secure the sale and to formalize it.

CONCLUSION

Now, if you put these three parts of the sales system in place in your business, you will be able to exit without exiting. You have to make sure that your sales team understands the four reasons why people buy and design your prospecting scripts on those four reasons. You also have to understand what a 20-Point Matrix is so that your sales team does not waste time on deals that aren't going to provide revenue.

Next, you have to make sure your sales team is following the Perfect Sales Sequence in order. If they go in talking about how great your company is out of the gate, this won't work. Let me tell you something… nobody cares. At the beginning of a process, the prospects need to know that you understand what's going on in their industry and their business.

This Perfect Sales Sequence will lead your sales team through a process and a system that will help you close twice as many sales as what you're closing now. Establishing systems and processes is the only way to leverage your time away from the business, while attaining more margin and getting the ideal life that you truly desire. You cannot fly by the seat of your pants anymore. You can't be the number one salesperson. You can't be the number one anything. You need to systematize, and this is exactly how you exit without exiting.

We'll take a look at the fourth core strategy in the next chapter.

9. INVEST IN PEOPLE

I love the CNBC show, *The Profit.* Marcus Lemonis is a fantastically successful entrepreneur, and this show is all about him going in and looking at an established business that's struggling with a specific aspect – profitability, marketing, manufacturing, production, retail, whatever it happens to be – and offering to partner with them to make it profitable. It is a reality show that documents his experience spending time on site at the business, meeting the owners and employees, analyzing the problems, and then investing his own money into the business to become a partner and help that business grow.

What I'm amazed at is how terrible some of the business owners treat their employees. Of course, treating people badly is good for reality television, but it's terrible for the reality of business! There are more than a few episodes where the owner literally cusses out one of the employees or berates the employee. At times, the owner talks on camera with the producer and with Marcus about how terrible some of the employees are. What astonishes me most is how these people are able to stay in business and why those employees continue to work for that company.

Let's look back at James' story from earlier in the book. Unlike many of the entrepreneurs on *The Profit*, James was a great employer. His employees loved and respected him and worked very hard to make his company successful. There is an old adage that says that your employees will never treat your customers any better than you treat your employees, and James took that to heart. James made his employees his number one priority by treating them well, giving them opportunities to grow, giving them recognition when they deserved it, and offering them a fair compensation plan. This is one of the reasons why when James decided to exit without exiting, it was easy for him to do so. He trusted his people. He knew they would step up and do the right thing even if he wasn't there monitoring their work each day. The mutual respect and trust he built with his employees paid great dividends.

As you read this chapter, you're going to see some unique tactics and strategies that James used to invest in his people. James wasn't special. He was just an average entrepreneur. He didn't have a weird connection or superpower that allowed him to get his employees to perform so well. Rather, James had a sincere trust in his people and the discipline to put certain "investment strategies" in place that helped him reap a great reward from their efforts. These strategies are easy to use and you can get similar results as well.

The fourth core strategy in the exit without exiting system is to **Invest in People**. I have a firm belief that your people are the most important part of your company. It's not you, it's not your customers – it's your people. I have known a few people who have pushed back on this idea that employees are most important. They assert that their customers are more important than employees, but I disagree with that. I think that the employees and the people in your company are the most important because without them, your company doesn't exist.

According to a *Forbes* article by Liz Ryan, "Five Reasons Why Employees Are More Important Than Customers" (*https://www.forbes.com/sites/lizryan/2016/11/01/five-reasons-*

employees-are-more-important-than-customers), there's data as to why this is true. Let's walk through each of these reasons and see what *Forbes* thinks.

WHY EMPLOYEES ARE MORE IMPORTANT THAN YOUR CUSTOMERS

Ryan says, "*Number one, every employee on your team has influence over some or all of your customer relationships. One disenchanted employee will crimp your ability to serve customers well, but lots of unhappy teammates will make it impossible for you to succeed. Whatever amount of time and energy you give to sales, marketing, and customer service, invest even more in keeping your team equipped, informed, and ready to rumble.*"

I wholeheartedly agree that your employees can influence your company in profound ways for better or for worse, which is why it's so vital to invest in them and to keep them motivated and ready to work hard for the good of the organization.

Ryan's second reason why employees are more important than customers is that, "*A toxic culture spreads its bad energy out beyond your company walls, into the community. Once your employer brand is trashed and your company becomes known as a toxic workplace, you'll have lost a critical, competitive advantage that could have powered your growth.*"

Again, I couldn't agree more. Toxic culture is detrimental to any company. Part of investing in your people is making sure that you're investing into the right culture so that your people feel valued, appreciated, and understood. You need to ensure that they get to share in the wins of the company. We'll talk about how to create a positive, productive culture later on in this chapter.

The third reason cited by Ryan is, "*Your employees have powerful energy to bring to your organization if you trust them enough to tap that fuel source. If you write job descriptions and believe that your employees are merely responsible for filling the tasks listed on their job descriptions, you're shooting too low in wasting time and money. If you empower your employees to use their excellent brains and hearts on the job, you will see them create breakthrough solutions, collaborate and innovate far beyond what you could have imagined. You will have created tremendous value for your company out of thin air, just by trusting yourself enough to trust the people that you hire."*

Notice she used the term *empower*. I even underlined it to make sure you didn't miss it. Recall the first core strategy in this program: Embrace Delegation. Delegation is *empowering* your employees to act on your behalf. So this claim reiterates and reinforces the importance of empowering employees to do what needs to get done. Don't limit them to your concepts and your ideas. The likelihood is that, if given the opportunity and some time to learn and grow, they will end up doing the tasks better than you did.

Ryan's fourth reason is, *"Your employees are the only real connection between a CEO and their leadership team at the top of an organization and the customers in the real world. If that connection is weak because the top managers don't trust their employees enough to listen to them, the leadership team will lose touch with its customers, and competitors will swoop in to take advantage of the situation. Listen to your employees."*

She's talking about a formal corporate structure here, but the same lesson applies across all businesses. Your employees are the touchstone of your company. If you're the CEO, you're likely not interacting with vendors, clients, and customers on a daily basis as much as your employees are – and this will especially be true when you exit without exiting. You have to listen to your employees to maintain that strong connection with them and what's going on in your business at all levels.

For the fifth reason, Ryan says, *"Every good thing that you hope to accomplish in your company will be powered by the same energy source, which is the commitment and talent of your employees. You cannot get that energy source if your employees are frustrated. When your culture is in danger, you have no higher priority than to open up communication and put things right."*

I love how she used the idea of your employees being a "power source." Your employees are in fact a power source for your company. They are what make things happen. Cash flow is king, yes, but employee culture in your business is actually going to be the operating system that makes your company run. It gives it the energy to do what needs to be done.

With all of these important reasons in mind, let's look at this fourth core strategy of investing in your employees. Let's start by asking a simple question: *What does it mean to invest in something?*

TWO WAYS TO INVEST

The word invest has two different meanings. Most people think of the one side, which is the financial investment. This means to put time and/or money to use in something offering potential profitable returns such as interest, income, or appreciation in value. From this financial perspective, investment simply means to put time or money into something for a potential profitable return.

But there's also another side of investing. Investing also means to furnish power, authority, or rank. So not only should you invest in your employees financially for the purpose of a profitable return, but you should also invest in them by empowering them. This goes back to embracing delegation. To empower your employees, you must furnish them with power, authority, rank, etc. Your people in your company are going to be your most important investment – bar none. If you invest properly, you will get a long term passive income as an owner-investor as opposed to just being an owner-operator.

Here's a short story of why I believe investing in people is so important. As I've mentioned before, I spent the first 13 years of my career in ministry. Part of what I did in ministry was to reiterate the teachings of Jesus to my church members. Jesus is quoted as saying the following statement in the book of Matthew:

"Do not lay up for yourselves treasures on earth, where moth and rust destroy and thieves break in and steal, but lay up for yourselves treasures in heaven, where neither moth nor rust destroys and where thieves do not break in and steal, for where your treasure is, there your heart will be also."

I always wondered what it meant. What did Jesus mean by "laying up treasures in heaven?" Does that mean we can't do anything about any treasures here on earth? Well, if you look up that word, the phrase "lay up" (or in some versions "to store up") it's the concept of investing. Jesus was saying, *"Hey, don't get too wrapped up in investing here on earth. I mean, you're going to lose this stuff. Money's not going to last. Gold's not going to last. None of this is going to last. Instead, store up or lay up to invest in eternity...in heaven."*

What confused me about this for years – even as a college-trained pastor with a degree in biblical studies – was how is one supposed to do that? Do you send your Bitcoins or your digital wallet address ahead to heaven? I mean, how do you do that? Of course, you can't. What is the only thing that transitions from this life to the next? People... that's it. In order to invest in heaven, in eternity, you have to invest in people because they're the only things that are going to make that transition. I know that some people don't share my spiritual beliefs, but as I've done all along, I can only share what I truly believe, which is that people are eternal and things are not. So this brought into perspective what it really means to invest.

Was Jesus saying, "*Don't invest in real estate, don't invest in cryptocurrencies, don't invest in gold?*" No. He was saying, *"Listen, your most important investment is going to be people."* What's interesting about this is that he finishes a statement by saying, *"For where your treasure is, there your heart will be also."* You can tell when you watch reality TV shows like *The Profit*, when the owner of the company is berating an employee, what does the employer really think about the employee? His treasure is not in that person. He's not investing in that person. They're only a means to an end.

What I teach my clients is that if you're going to free yourself up from the daily obligations of running a business and being in the weeds every day, one of the most important things you have to do – one of the four core strategies – is investing in people. That means you must put in the time and/or money into them for the purpose of a profitable return. Every employee – and I've been very clear about this with all the employees who work for me – is an investment for me. I'm investing in them financially for the purpose of a return. Certainly there are different metrics for different employees, different levels of employees, different companies, but the reality is if I can't get a minimum of $3 in profitability back from what I spend on an investment in my company, including employees, then it's probably not a good investment.

Employees need to understand that I'm investing in them financially for the purpose of a financial return. I also want to invest in them to furnish them with power, authority, and rank to act on my behalf so that I don't have to be there. This investment not only gets me a financial return, but it gets me more of the non-renewable resource we spoke about in Chapter 3, which is time. Time is the thing I'm most interested in, much more than money. Of course, my business has to produce profit ("money") or it isn't worth doing in the first place. Once I get the money flowing in, my next goal is always to figure out how to get as much time as possible. Investing in your people will get you money AND time.

FOUR WAYS TO INVEST IN PEOPLE

There are many different ways to invest in people. I'm going to focus on what I feel are the four most powerful ways to do so.

#1) Hire the Right People

The first way is to hire the right people. A mantra I've espoused for a very long time that I will admit is much easier to say than it is to practice, is: "Hire Slow. Fire Fast." That means your hiring process needs to be slow so that you can find the right person to bring on board. Then, the firing process should be quick and painless. You need to get it over with as quickly as possible. Generally speaking, if you've already thought that you should fire somebody, by the time you think about it and mull over it, you should have already done it.

I've had clients of mine who've confided in me in our coaching sessions that they're thinking about firing so-and-so, or they're thinking about letting somebody go, and I tell them, *"Hey, if you've already thought that you're probably already way past the date that it should have happened, and you need to go ahead and do it."* Without any exceptions, every time one of my clients delays firing somebody and then ultimately ends up firing them, they tell me that they wish they'd done it when they first thought about it.

Of course, ideally you won't have to fire very often because you've taken the time to hire the best people for the right roles and tasks. Firing someone is not a fun thing. I remember the very first person I ever had to fire. I really didn't want to do it. We knew we should have fired her a long time before we did, as she just was not a good fit culturally. She clearly felt entitled and was causing problems. She questioned my authority. Everything about the situation was wrong, and we knew that we should let her go before we did. Then, when we got to the place where we were actually going to finally let her go, I was too chicken to do it! I ended up having my business partner do it for me, which is not what I would ever recommend you do. However, that's when I started to learn the lesson of hiring slowly and firing fast.

For you to better learn from my past mistakes, I want to share 10 steps to find, hire, and onboard new team members. You can

download this list as a resource to use in your office.
therealjasonduncan.com/hiring

I'm going to give all 10 steps without going into detail here. Then, you can take a look at the PDF document for a deeper dive into each one.

1. Write an ad.
2. Create an application form.
3. Post your ad.
4. Review the applications.
5. Conduct phone calls.
6. Conduct in-person interviews and give a pre-employment assessment.
7. Conduct a culture check.
8. Make the offer.
9. Sign the employment agreement.
10. Welcome and onboard your new team member.

If you follow these 10 steps, you will not only find better team members, you'll be able to hire and onboard team members and keep them longer. To give you an example, I've used a version of this for the last 12 years of owning companies, and for the most part, I've only had to fire two or three people that didn't fit because I broke my own rules and didn't follow this process. Everyone else that I have hired through the right system (using these 10 steps) has stayed with me for years. I have people that have been with me for nearly a decade who shouldn't stay at companies as long as they do, but are still with me because I've hired them correctly and invested in them the right way.

#2) Delegate Appropriately

The next way to invest in people is to delegate appropriately. We talked about this extensively in Chapter 6, so I'm not going to go into it all again here. However, I will just remind you that delegating appropriately means you don't confiscate their roles back, nor do you abdicate the responsibility of making sure that it's done correctly. Also, make sure you seek their input on creating systems and processes so they will have more authority moving forward, which allows for an easier exit without exiting.

#3) Stay Laser Focused on Culture

Building the proper culture can lead you to success as you exit, or it can lead you to failure as you attempt to exit. Culture is so incredibly important that it requires as much attention as you can give to it.

Here's a tip:

There is a sociological and psychological phenomenon known as the "Power of 10%." What this tells us is that 10% of any group can sway the other 90%. It doesn't take a majority to make it happen. Essentially, this says that when 10% of any group start believing or behaving a certain way, that 10% will soon become the majority. This isn't just based on anecdotal evidence. Scientists at Rensselaer Polytechnic Institute actually concluded that it only takes 10% of a population holding an unshakable belief in order to convince the majority to adopt that same belief. In fact, scientists have found that this will always be the case. *"When the number of committed opinion holders is below 10%, there is no visible progress in the spread of ideas. It would literally take the amount of time comparable to the age of the universe for this size group to reach the majority,"* said SCNARC Director, Boleslaw Szymanski, the Claire and Roland Schmitt Distinguished Professor at Rensselaer. *"Once that number grows above 10%, the idea spreads like a flame."*

What we saw during the COVID pandemic and what we've seen during riots and uprisings is that it doesn't take more than about 10% of a group to start flipping cars over and smashing windows before the entire mob is doing it. That's how mob mentality works. It doesn't require 50%. It doesn't require 60% or 70%. It only requires 10%. The rest will follow.

What this tells us as employers and as entrepreneurs is that we must invest in our people and pay attention to them. If there becomes a 10% that is behaving or acting a specific way, which becomes negative to our overall culture, that could end up swaying the entire group. Let me give you an example from James' experience.

James had an employee named Cory who worked for him in his operations department. Cory was a great employee in terms of output and productivity. He did his job well. He looked for new and better ways to do things. He executed correctly, and he was very good with customers. The issue was that Cory was somewhat of a negative person. James thought of him as a "Negative Nelly," which is someone who is negative, doesn't look at the bright side of things, and is always complaining. Every time James had internal meetings, or a sit down session with Cory individually, he would bring a negative perspective. There was always something that wasn't right, and that was causing more of a problem than James realized. He addressed it a couple of times, but it didn't seem to make any difference. It grew to become much more of a problem. James figured that it wasn't a big deal and rationalized the fact that he was negative, because Cory was very good at his job. Eventually, James had to fire Cory. He sensed that the negativity was bad for morale and thought it was best to let Cory go and find a replacement. He had finally conceded that Cory's negativity outweighed his productivity. The day after Cory was no longer an employee, one of James' top employees came to him with tears in his eyes. He shut the door to James' office as he walked in and said, *"I need to talk to you."*

James had no idea what was going on. He lost Cory, whom he now had to replace, and now he had one of his top employees, Phil, coming to him in tears. *"What's up?"* James asked, nervous about what the response might be. Phil looked at James, tears still in his eyes, and said, *"I was about to resign. I have my resignation letter with me,"* he said, motioning to the piece of paper in his right hand. Phil continued, *"And I was about to give it to you. I couldn't take Cory's negative attitude anymore. You have no idea how much his attitude affected all of us around here. We really liked him as a person and he did his job well, as you know, but dammit his attitude sucked. It was rubbing off on everyone. I was ready to quit just to get away from all of this negativity, but now that he's gone I'm going to stay."*

James was totally blown away. He had no idea that Cory had such a negative impact, even on one of his best employees.

Thankfully, James' best employee didn't leave, and he's still with the company to this day. James dodged a bullet, and it woke him up to the importance of culture within his company. Over the next week or two, James started paying attention to people's attitudes around the office, how meetings were going, and more. He detected a significant and unmistakable uptick in people's productivity, their happiness around the office, and their general attitude. One day, he pulled a few employees aside one by one and asked if they noticed this positivity around the office. They all said that they absolutely did. When he asked what they thought the reason was, without fail or without trying to be spiteful, they all said, *"Well, ever since Cory left, we just feel like we can be more free to talk because we're not being shot down every time we come up with an idea."*

At that time, James had 11 employees. Cory was one employee, so the measurement remains correct in regards to that 10% mark. Cory was having a negative effect on the rest of James' company, and he didn't even understand how big of a negative effect it was until he was gone. As a leader, you have to make sure you are laser focused on culture. Always keep your culture front and center in all aspects, because the power of 10% is 100% true.

WHAT IS CULTURE?

You might be asking at this point, what exactly is culture? Culture encompasses the unspoken rules of how we act, how we treat one another, and how we show up for work. For founders and entrepreneurs, you dictate and control culture until you have about 20 employees. Once you get past 20-25 employees, the culture starts taking on a life of its own based on what was established by you when the company had less employees. As the founder, you will have less and less control over the group as a whole. This is why it's so important to pay attention to culture right out of the gate, and as you start establishing your business in the first couple of years. Once it's established, you can pull back and know that the culture will maintain in your absence.

One of the things that I did as a culture initiative in my company was to implement a monthly "family meal." We would shut the office down one Friday per month. All of the employees would meet in our training room for a team meeting. All of the Directors and Vice Presidents would give short reports on what was going on inside the company, because, as you know, often someone in one department doesn't know what's going on in another. Each department director would give a report, and I would do some form of training as the CEO on a topic that would be encouraging and motivational. I would also make sure to review our company culture initiatives to reinforce them. Then, we would have lunch. We'd cater in for lunch, or we'd do a potluck. We prohibited phones and business talk during this time so that we could share a meal together and enjoy each other's company. One or two people would be selected ahead of time to come up with some sort of group activity that promoted team building, and we would do this together after lunch. There were times where we played games such as adult versions of Jenga, Connect Four, or Two Truths and a Lie. Other times, we'd have a cornhole tournament with prizes. Our monthly family meal was one of the initiatives that helped develop and nurture a company culture I was proud of. As soon as lunch and the games were over, the work day was done. Everyone got paid for a full day, but only worked for a fraction of it. Then, they all were able to go home early for a long weekend.

It's important to state that just because it wasn't our most productive day businesswise, we didn't let people take that day off to get an extended weekend. Everyone was required to be present. We made the whole team come in because we thought that it was extremely important for everyone to be there in order to build a stronger, more cohesive, and ultimately more productive group.

Another culture initiative we put in place is to make sure that every salaried employee got unlimited paid time off ("PTO"). Hourly employees got a different PTO plan, and when we first decided to implement this policy, we were somewhat anxious. What if people take advantage of it? Instead, what we found was that people want freedom and choices. Just like you as an entrepreneur, your employees want freedom and choices as much as you do. Having only a week or two of vacation annually really doesn't give them freedom and choices to travel and go do what they want to do. So giving them unlimited PTO allows them to take as much time off as possible – with a couple of caveats.

The first caveat is that you still have to make a request for time off, and it still has to be approved by your manager. Caveat two is that the work that you are required to complete still must be completed. That doesn't mean we are asking you or making you work while you're on vacation – quite the contrary. It just means that you have a plan to make sure that your tasks are taken care of while you're gone. Your plan to exit without exiting – working in your business only 10 hours a week – won't work out if you don't plan well and put measures in place to make sure everything is accomplished correctly in your absence, right? In like manner, this unlimited PTO concept won't work unless employees appropriately plan for their time off and make sure their jobs are handled in their absence. Now, if an employee wants to take a week off at the beach and brings a laptop in order to maintain email communications with vendors or customers while away, that's the employee's choice. Although, I actually encourage people not to do any work while they're on vacation. As a matter of fact, one of my employees went on his first vacation in three years after he started working for me, and I told him he was prohibited from taking his work laptop. At first, he was really apprehensive about not having his laptop so he could check in.

But when he got back, he said, "Boss, that was one of the most enjoyable, relaxing times I've had in 10 years."

With caveat number two, I found the freedom to choose to take time off empowered each employee to take great care to train their coworkers on things that needed to be attended to while they were on vacation. If they did so, their tasks were covered while they were away. It helped the entire team perform better and the employee actually got to enjoy their vacation without feeling like they either (A) had to work on vacation or (B) would have to walk back into a huge pile of to-dos when they got back. I'm a huge proponent of unlimited PTO as long as it is structured and managed correctly.

Ultimately, I want to make sure that people understand their time off is their time off, but they have to make sure that their job gets done in their absence. This helps pass along the whole idea of delegation, so I delegate to them and they now learn how to delegate to other people to make sure that their job is completed even when they're on PTO.

A final cultural initiative I want to talk about is something I call the "Five Pillars of Excellence." It is my belief that we should commit to excellence in everything that we do, and in my various companies, we know that just being acceptable is not acceptable. We don't just do it to be good enough. We want to make sure that we're excellent in all that we do.

I talk about this with our employees in terms of the present and future – that is, where are we today versus where we want to be in the future? What is our vision for the future? We want to be known as the most excellent company in this industry doing X, Y, or Z. If we're going to build a bridge from where we are today to where we want to go, we have to make sure that the pillars we build that bridge with are solid. And these are pillars of excellence.

Pillars matter immensely to the structural integrity of any bridge, but unfortunately, pillars aren't very often noticed. That is, until they fail. Such was the case in Minneapolis, Minnesota, on the evening of August 1, 2007. Slow moving traffic crawled along the I-35 West bridge during peak rush hour, as it had done countless times before. However, at 6:05 PM on the dot, the unthinkable happened. Drivers on the bridge recalled hearing a beam snap, followed by a loud clunk. Then, they felt the bridge begin to tremble. Within seconds, a thousand feet of the bridge collapsed and about 456 feet of the main span fell 108 feet down into the Mississippi River below. Thirteen people were killed, and 145 people were injured as a result.

The cause of the collapse was related to the fact that the pillars of the bridge were not built or maintained properly. While certainly less tragic, the same thing can happen in our businesses. If we don't properly build the bridge from today, to where we want to go in the future on the right pillars, it could collapse and people could be harmed. A failed business often wreaks havoc on your life and the lives of the employees and their families.

In my 10-Hour Entrepreneur course *(ExitWithoutExiting.com)*, I teach about the Five Pillars of Excellence in our companies. Here are the five pillars of excellence I have instituted in my companies.

Excellence in Culture
Excellence in Data Management
Excellence in Cost Management
Excellence in Communication
Excellence in Service

WHAT IS EXCELLENCE IN CULTURE?

For us, excellence in culture boils down to three things: (1) Always act with integrity, treating others the way we would like to be treated. (2) Always be enthusiastic, giving our very best at all times. (3) Always be learning new ways to improve your performance and knowledge.

As you ponder these things, consider what a company built on this pillar of excellence in culture would feel like... mutual respect, enthusiasm, and a growth mindset. These things will produce a great company culture if adhered to regularly and unwaveringly by each employee, beginning with you as the CEO.

WHAT IS EXCELLENCE IN DATA MANAGEMENT?

Excellence in data management means that we will (1) always keep detailed records, (2) always keep data organized and accessible, and (3) always protect sensitive data.

It goes without saying that the future of business is built on data. The biggest companies on earth are in the data business. If you want to build an excellent company, you must manage and maintain data with excellence. When this is done – and every employee recognizes the importance of data--the culture in the business can focus on something that matters more than simply making a buck. Employees will take better notes, record data more accurately, store data correctly, and protect sensitive data from falling into the wrong hands.

WHAT IS EXCELLENCE IN COST MANAGEMENT?

Cost management isn't only about *your* costs. It's about the customer's costs as well. For us, this boils down to three things: (1) Always make decisions that maximize financial savings for both the company and the customer without sacrificing quality or safety. (2) Always look for cost-reduction strategies in how we operate the company. (3) Always pay attention to how every action affects the bottom line of the company and how that affects opportunities for increased salaries over time.

Being bottom-line-focused is important because it helps everyone pay attention to how their actions affect the company. It is not enough for you and your upper management to understand how every action of the company correlates to bottom line profitability. Imagine the difference in your business when your administrative assistant, your service workers, and your sales people understand how each action affects the bottom line? Cost management is a very important pillar.

WHAT IS EXCELLENCE IN COMMUNICATION?

How we communicate is vital to the future of our businesses. Here are three ways I encourage excellence in communication: (1) Always be positive, professional, and courteous. (2) Always communicate clearly and concisely. (3) Always project excellence in the company brand.

Negativity can kill company culture, as we painfully saw in James' story that I told earlier in this chapter. Therefore, encouraging excellence in communication reinforces how our attitudes and the ways in which we communicate will affect the business long term. Do not underestimate the importance and power of proper communication in your business.

WHAT IS EXCELLENCE IN SERVICE?

Serving your customers is vital to maintaining profitability long term. As I have stressed excellence in service to my teams, here are three things I focus on: (1) Always seek the best interest of all parties. (2) Always do it right the first time without cutting corners. (3) Always admit to and correct mistakes immediately.

I'll share a quick story with you about how this played out at one of my companies. I had one of my employees come to me privately to tell me that she had made a mistake on a job. As she explained to me the mistake that she made, she went on to say that she took time to go back and admit the mistake to the customer and offered to fix it on the spot, even though it was going to cost us some extra money we hadn't budgeted for in the project.

She understood that we were committed to excellence in service, so this seemed like the right thing to do. Rather than scolding her for the mistake and the extra money we had to spend to fix her mistake, I commended her actions and thanked her for her commitment to excellence in service. At the next family meal, I shared that story with everyone and told them how she had screwed up. They were shocked at first, thinking I was calling her out in front of everyone. But then, when I explained how she handled her screw-up, everyone's eyes lit up and applause broke out around the room. Everyone understood that this was an example of excellence in service. It is an important pillar upon which we will continue to build our company.

The way you build your pillars of excellence may be different than mine, but I highly recommend using some sort of visual illustration of these pillars of excellence throughout your company. I created posters and hung them in our training room, break room, and other strategic places around the office. They weren't just to make me feel good as the owner, they were constant reminders of how we are committed to excellence in all things. We made sure to review them in each meeting and talk about them constantly. If you want to create your own pillars of excellence, there is a free resource on my website at this link (*therealjasonduncan.com/5pillars*) that you can use to download my Five Pillars of Excellence as a template for you to create your own.

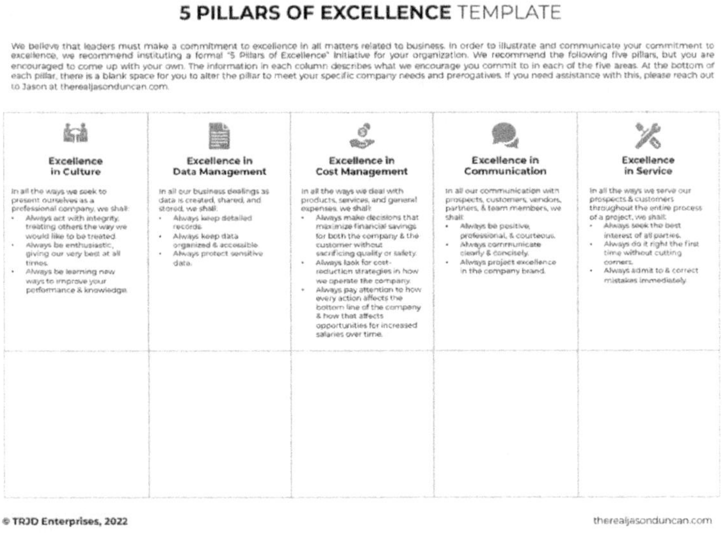

5 PILLARS OF EXCELLENCE TEMPLATE

We believe that leaders must make a commitment to excellence in all matters related to business. In order to illustrate and communicate your commitment to excellence, we recommend instituting a formal "5 Pillars of Excellence" Initiative for your organization. We recommend the following five pillars, but you are encouraged to come up with your own. The information in each column describes what we encourage you commit to in each of the five areas. At the bottom of each pillar, there is a blank space for you to alter the pillar to meet your specific company needs and prerogatives. If you need assistance with this, please reach out to Jason at therealjasonduncan.com.

Excellence in Culture	Excellence in Data Management	Excellence in Cost Management	Excellence in Communication	Excellence in Service
In all the ways we seek to present ourselves as a professional company, we shall: • Always act with integrity, treating others the way we would like to be treated. • Always be enthusiastic, giving our very best at all times. • Always be learning new ways to improve your performance & knowledge.	In all our business dealings as data is created, shared, and stored, we shall: • Always keep detailed records. • Always keep data organized & accessible. • Always protect sensitive data.	In all the ways we deal with products, services, and general expenses, we shall: • Always make decisions that maximize financial savings for both the company & the customer without sacrificing quality or safety. • Always look for cost-reduction strategies in how we operate the company. • Always pay attention to how every action affects the bottom line of the company & how that affects opportunities for increased salaries over time.	In all our communication with prospects, customers, vendors, partners, & team members, we shall: • Always be positive, professional, & courteous. • Always communicate clearly & concisely. • Always project excellence in the company brand.	In all the ways we serve our prospects & customers throughout the entire process of a project, we shall: • Always seek the best interest of all parties. • Always do it right the first time without cutting corners. • Always admit to & correct mistakes immediately.

© TRJD Enterprises, 2022 therealjasonduncan.com

Image 5.1

Now, let's move on to the final way I want to focus on investing in people – the financial side.

INVEST FINANCIALLY

Let me ask you a question. Can you assign greater responsibility for running day-to-day operations and increase your employees' pay? Is there a way to do that? If so, then you should. Think about time and money. Which one do you want more of?

As we discussed earlier in the book, time is a non-renewable resource, meaning once you spend it you can never get it back. Money, on the other hand, is a renewable resource. It's a resource that once you spend, you can get back. Many entrepreneurs give away hours of their time just trying to get money. Very few spend money to get time, but it's the latter who win and who are successful. To me, that is an investment worth making. I believe that you should always invest in renewable resources to get non-renewable resources. In other words, spend money to get time. Don't spend time getting money. Let me give you an example.

When I began the exit from my company at the end of 2019 and into 2020, I made a decision to take $80,000 out of my personal take home pay as the founder and CEO of the company and distribute that to four key people in my organization. To be clear, this was coming out of my pocket, not the bottom line of the company, which was already paying my salary. In return for this large raise, I said, *"Listen, I'm going to give you this big raise, but I need each of you to step up. I'm going to give you vice president titles, and I want you to take care of the day-to-day operations. First, I'm going to check in once a week with you. Then, I'm going to move to checking in once a month, then once a quarter, and then just once a year."* And that's exactly what I did.

When I told my wife that my annual salary would be reduced by $80,000, she was a bit worried at first. But like all investments, you have to spend money to make money. I was willing to invest that $80,000 in my employees in order to make more money later. Not only did I make more than that later, I ended up getting so much more time back that I was able to use productively to create even more financial opportunities for myself.

You might not be able to do that financially. You may say, *"Hey, I don't have $80,000 of my personal take home pay that I can reinvest into my employees."* That's completely fine. The exact dollar amount is not the point. What you need to be thinking about is, what can you do? Is there a way that you can say to a key employee or two, *"Listen, we're earning X number of dollars every year for this other thing. I'm going to pull that back. I'm going to give that to you because I want you to take a bigger role in managing day-to-day operations. Why? Because I want to step away from day-to-day operations. I've got some other things I need to focus on as the CEO and the founder. I want to make sure that I'm focusing on what's most important for the longevity of the business."*

When you do that, you have to make sure that you get a buy-in. You have to test their abilities, and you have to turn over authority slowly and methodically. You can't just say, *"Hey, you're in charge. Have fun!"* and walk away. Remember that's abdication, not delegation. I promise if you make these types of investments in your people, the long-term returns will far outweigh any short-term losses or anxiety. Investing in people is crucial to your exit without exiting.

10. TIMELINE TO EXIT WITHOUT EXITING

A question I get asked about in terms of the exit lifestyle and the entire exit without exiting process is: how long does it take? Of course, this comes from a different perspective, depending upon where you are in your process, business, and life. Some people are asking that because they're in a hurry. Other people ask because they're simply curious, and others are planners who want to make sure that they can schedule out their eventual exit. As a reminder, I want to let you know that every single entrepreneur will exit their business at some point, whether voluntarily or involuntarily. You could choose to shut it down, choose to sell it, or choose to exit without exiting. You can also not choose. In that instance, you could go bankrupt. You could die. You could be sick and incapacitated. Whatever the scenario is, you will in fact exit.

Edward, Cheryl, and James were all able to pull off their respective exits to varying degrees of success, but on wildly different timelines. Edward never really thought about exiting at all until he was completely burned out. By then, there was no quick or easily recognizable path to a successful exit. It took him about four months before he was able to list his business for sale, and then it took him 18 months to find a buyer willing to purchase it at an agreeable price. It then took another six months to work through the asset purchase agreement. Furthermore, as you remember, the buyer required Edward to stick around for three more years as a condition of the sale. So all in, it took Edward almost five and half years from when he decided he wanted to exit until he was actually "free" from his business.

Cheryl's exit timeline was a bit quicker than Edward's. She made the decision that she wanted to sell after her seventh year in business. That was the first year that she took a family vacation since starting the business. She had been so busy for so long, she never took the time to take a vacation. After the one week trip to the beach with her family, she had a realization that she was missing too many important events in her personal life. On the flight back home, she decided to begin preparing her business for sale.

But as most workaholics know, making a decision and following through on it are two very different things. Although Cheryl had decided to prepare the business for exit after that trip, she really didn't make any significant changes in the business for another two years. She was in the middle of a large customer acquisition and threw herself fully into that deal, working 70 and sometimes 80 hours a week to secure this new customer. After her ninth anniversary in the business, she had a broker list her business for sale. It only took six months to find a buyer and another six months to work on the asset purchase agreement. So all in, it took Cheryl about three years to get "free" from her business after making the decision to exit.

James never wanted to sell his business at all. In the beginning he worked very long hours to get the business established and make sure that the systems, processes, and people were in place to generate predictable revenue. Before long, his business became a cash-flow machine that provided him and his family the lifestyle they enjoyed. The first two years were like any startup. He worked long hours and put in a lot of effort. Then in the third year, he began making the changes necessary to allow him to get out of the daily operations. An "exit" per se, wasn't really on his mind. He just wanted to enjoy lots of time with his young kids and his wife.

For James, he was only working 10 hours a week in the business by the fourth year. At the five-year mark, James was only checking on his business about 10 hours per month. His "exit" had happened slowly and almost imperceptibly. Because he had planned all along for his business to be a self-sustaining entity, James was free from without having to make any major adjustments or looking for a buyer. This is what exit without exiting is all about.

PLANNING IS CRITICAL

As mentioned in Chapter 5, I had the pleasure of interviewing Dr. Sascha Becker of Monash University in Australia on my podcast. If you remember, what they discovered after studying what happened to businesses whose founders died was alarming: each business saw a significant and permanent decrease in revenue and profitability. Specifically, there was a 60% decline in revenue and a 36% reduction in profit for the businesses that remained open. One difference they discovered was that those who planned for the exiting of the founder (Note: this type of planning often occurred when the founder was known to be dying) were able to sustain the business longer and their losses weren't as large.

What that tells me, and what it should tell you, is that planning matters, and planners are the ones who are going to be able to accelerate an exit from the business faster than anybody else. James' exit happened quickly and without much fanfare because he planned for it. Edward's was slow and painful because he hadn't planned for it. So, the very fact that you're wondering how long this would take is a good sign; you're already starting to formulate the seeds of a plan!

The short answer to how long it takes to exit your company and become a "10-hour entrepreneur" like James – if you're serious and you plan well – is under a year. Even so, you need to embrace the four core principles we've talked about in this book. To illustrate the process, let me tell you about how long it took me to exit.

It began during a meeting with my business coach in 2018. He asked, "What do you want out of your future?" One of the things I knew I wanted was to get out of day-to-day operations. The only way that I thought I could do that was by selling the company. We spent another meeting or two going through my options. One of the big questions was this: Is the option of selling the business even viable? Ultimately, we discovered that it wasn't. The reason it wasn't viable was because I had positioned myself at the center of the business. Everything revolved around me; therefore the business was not worth as much as it would've been had I, like James, had systems in place to allow it to run on its own. Basically, the business would have been far more valuable had I been doing all of the things I've talked about in this book like having a plan, and having been following the four principles of the exit without exiting method at the time.

YOU CAN EXIT WITHOUT EXITING – WITHOUT SELLING!

Once I accepted the idea that I couldn't sell it right then, it took me about 18 months to arrange my business in such a way that I didn't have to be present every single day. I didn't start this process with the intent to get everything in order so that I could sell it. I started with the intent to figure out specifically if there was a way that I could still get out of day-to-day operations, still make the income that I was used to, still have the tax benefits, but not sell the company. I realize that a lot of people who are in the mergers and acquisition space and who coach how to exit businesses, will teach you that it takes three to five years to prepare a business for sale. I would agree with that. Both Edward's and Cheryl's stories illustrate this truth. I also have many colleagues, attorneys, and friends who would agree with this rule of thumb that you have to plan for a sale three to five years prior to the sale occurring.

One of the reasons it takes so long is that your accounting has to be razor sharp. Your books have to be completely on point. Everything must be perfect, and let's be honest: as much as we all want our books to be accurate and easy to understand, the day-to-day grind of running operations sometimes dulls our focus on making the books razor sharp. We don't do anything illegal or unethical, mind you, but we might cut some corners here and there. A few too many "Ask Accountant" entries, or more than a few "Uncategorized Income" entries. Things like that work for us to keep the business going from month to month, but they will ruin your valuation. Buyers want to see a crystal clear picture of the financial reality of your business.

It wasn't my intent to sell when I started my process. I just wanted to get down to 10 hours or less per week spent in the business. I was trying to figure out how to get out of the day-to-day, not how to make my books look perfect for a potential buyer. This is another reason why this exit without exiting method is so great. You can get to the exit lifestyle much sooner than the three to five year timeline it would normally take to prepare your books and your business for sale.

For example, I'm in the process of purchasing a business right now, and the sellers have been working on getting this business ready to sell for several years. As a matter of fact, it's been on the market for well over a year. We are under a letter of intent and I'm in the due diligence phase, scrutinizing every aspect of their business. And you know what? They have everything in order. Their books are in order. Their tax returns are in order. Everything is ready because they took a long time to prepare for it because they were looking to sell.

On the other hand, if you don't want to sell it, but you do want to exit day-to-day operations, you can do that much faster because you're not trying to shore up your books. That is not to say that you shouldn't be trying to make sure that your books are correct and accurate. But it is to say that you don't have to worry about correcting every little honest mistake or discrepancy as you would if you were trying to sell.

FIVE FACTORS THAT AFFECT TIMELINE

Here are the five factors that will affect how quickly your exit without exiting timeline will be realized. I'll list them and talk about each of them separately. Remember that what I'm talking about here is NOT the timeline for a total exit. Rather, I'm going to show you the factors that affect your timeline in order to exit without exiting.

ANNUAL REVENUE

What does annual revenue have to do with your timeline and the exit lifestyle? Let's look at this in revenue tiers.

A business that's doing under $500,000 is going to take about 18-24 months, not because it would be an overly complex mission but because you likely don't have enough cash necessary to get the systems and people organized and ready to take over your business. If you're doing less than $500,000 in annual revenue, you are likely doing everything yourself. Your timeline will be extended because you have to hire, onboard, and train employees. You then have to have the runway and financial ability to hire those people. So, your timeline will be somewhere between 18-24 months before you'd be able to exit without exiting.

If you're doing between $500,000 and $1 million, your timeline is still going to be right at about a year. Again, you don't have a ton of resources available to hire those people, and you probably don't have enough capital to do everything you need to do in order to have you replaced in the business on a day-to-day basis.

Next, if you're doing between $1 million and $5 million, your timeline is going to be in the three to four quarters range for exiting without exiting. You should have enough cash flow to put systems and processes in place in order to offset your daily running of the business.

If you're making more than $5 million, your timeline as it relates to revenue will be much shorter because you are likely to have the capital resources available in order to accelerate your specific exit personally. At this point, it will be about how good your company culture is and the team you've put in place. Essentially, that will dictate your overall timeline. If you have built a great team and have a great culture, you could be down to "10-hour entrepreneur" status in as little as six months.

NUMBER OF EMPLOYEES

The second factor is the number of employees, which relates a lot to your annual revenue but doesn't always correlate exactly. That's why I discuss this idea separately. Again, let's look at this in terms of tiers. If you have no employees, it will take you much longer to exit without exiting than if you have many employees. When you have no employees, you're doing everything yourself and acting as a "single shingle" person as they say. This in turn makes your timeline longer. You have to find an employee, hire an employee, train an employee, and then be able to trust them in order to turn things over. You're going to be very hard pressed to pull that off in a year. In fact, it may take you 18 to 24 months to do this successfully.

If you have 10 or more employees, you should be able to do this in a year or under, because you should have the number of employees required to offset your daily operational work. If you embrace delegation, just as we talked about in Chapter 6, your ability to exit should be swift and relatively painless. This is provided that you have the right people working for you already.

AGE OF YOUR BUSINESS

The third factor in determining how quickly you can get to the exit lifestyle is the age of your business. If your business is relatively new – just like with employees and revenue – you're going to take longer to exit because you likely haven't had the time to develop your own self-sufficient systems yet. You're still figuring them out for yourself, much less being able to turn them over to other people in order to operate on your behalf.

If your business is mature and has been around for a long time, but you've been the center of that business since day one, then you too are going to have a hard time accelerating this timeline. It's going to take you at least a year to make this happen, because it will take time to disentangle yourself from the daily operations and get people comfortable with the idea that you're not going to be there every single day. You might have created a monster in many ways, if your business is old and you've been at the center of it for the whole time.

However, if your business is anywhere from five to ten years old, you're going to be able to accomplish this in under a year, assuming the other factors are favorable. You likely have enough age and brand recognition in the marketplace. People know who you are, and they understand that the business is not 100% relying on your personality and your ability to get things done. Therefore, you should be able to accelerate the exit.

SYSTEMS IN PLACE

The fourth factor refers to the systems that you've already put in place. If you have spent a considerable amount of time and you've been systematized up to this point, you're going to accelerate your exit much quicker than anyone who's not done so. For example, if you already have a good sales system in place, a customer onboarding system, systems for your vendors and your contractors who do work for you or sell your product, then it's going to be much easier to exit because you're not creating everything from scratch.

I encourage you to sit down with your employees and go through your current systems to see where there are holes and where there are improvements that can accelerate your timeline to exit. If you have no systems, you still can exit in about 12-18 months. Although true, you will have to be utterly committed to putting systems and processes in place as soon as possible, specifically in regards to sales. You have to make sure that area is correct. Remember to always ask for buy-in and input from your employees early in the systematizing process. You don't want to create something that's void of other people's opinions, especially if those other people are going to be performing the tasks and duties to make things happen. Overall, the number of systems you currently have in place will have a lot to do with whether or not you'll be able to succeed quickly in exiting.

PERSONAL MANAGEMENT STYLE

The fifth factor has everything to do with your personal management style. Believe it or not, micromanagement – even though we look at it today as a very negative thing – was an actual management style put in place by the Japanese automotive industry in the late 1970s. They would closely watch every single thing that the employees did without allowing them freedom to make their own decisions. This micromanagement system actually increased productivity and quality.

While I'm not recommending micromanagement on a wide scale, there is a place for it when you are preparing your business for the exit. For example, Jeff Bezos, Elon Musk, Steve Jobs, and Bill Gates are very well-known micromanagers. They might not have paid attention to every little detail a hundred percent of the time, but they did at specific times and for specific processes in relation to certain projects. Like these men, your own management style will be a factor in determining how quickly you're able to get out of your business. If you need to micromanage a certain process or system as a part of your exit plan, then by all means you should do it.

But if you are micromanaging when it's not helping your company, it's instead going to hinder your exit process and take longer for you to become extricated from the middle of the business. On the other hand, if your management style is too loose or too hands off, that might be hindering your business and timeline in regards to the exit, as well. In fact, this may increase the amount of time needed to get you out of the day-to-day operations, because a very loose management style may also mean that you don't have the proper systems put in place. Then, everyone is making their own decisions all the time, which means there is no predictable outcome. In this case, you're losing money and profitability is probably low. Revenue is being drained, because there aren't systems that are being followed, and you're not enforcing those systems.

If you're in the middle ground, somewhere between micromanagement and loose management, you would expect to be able to exit your business in about a year or less. This is because people trust you, and you trust them. There's discipline put in place when you have a management style that is setting you up for success. Of course, these five factors must be observed in concert in order to accurately predict your timeline regarding your exit. You simply cannot assume that just because you are doing $10 million in revenue that you can exit in under a year. If you are a terrible micromanager, this simply won't happen. As you can see, these factors must all align in order for your exit to work more quickly.

Having learned about the five factors that affect the exit timeline, the question to ask yourself is where are you in terms of these five categories? How do you factor into each of these five categories? Where is your revenue? How many employees do you have? How old is your business? What systems do you already have in place? What is your personal management style? Answering those five questions and knowing where you are in the steps will indicate whether or not you're going to be on the short or the long end of getting yourself to the exit lifestyle.

TIMELINE ADVICE FOR LICENSED PROFESSIONALS

I want to mention the timeline for licensed entrepreneurs, because it comes up quite frequently. Dentists, lawyers, doctors, chiropractors, accountants – people who have to have a license or some sort of certification to do their job – fall into this category. A friend of mine who was on my podcast (episode #065), The Root of All Success, was a very successful chiropractor in New York. When I interviewed Dr. JC Doornick, he told me about how he used to work 70, 80, and 90 hour weeks in his chiropractic practice even though he had another chiropractor who worked for him. The business was going really well, but he was overworked and he wasn't enjoying it. His health was terrible, and he didn't have any passion for life. "This wasn't what I thought entrepreneurship would be," he admitted.

He was unexpectedly presented with an opportunity to start another business, so he started paying attention to his "free time." Eventually, his other business started exceeding the income that he was making through his chiropractic business. Rather than going through the process of selling the business, he just gave it to the other chiropractor. No sale occurred – he just gave it away. Now, he regrets it in some sense, but what he doesn't regret is how blessed the person is who took over the practice. It also gave him the freedom to go do what he wanted to do when he exited. While I wouldn't recommend this, and he wouldn't recommend it either, that is one way for licensed people to exit their business.

Another chiropractor friend of mine, Dr. Justin Moseley, had a successful practice and wanted to get out of the daily operations. He was able to get his business running with other licensed chiropractors so well that he could walk away without having to give the business away, or even selling it. What I would say to those of you who are reading this who are licensed is that maybe you're an attorney, a lawyer, a CPA, or a dentist. You could be thinking, "Well, how do I get out of this business? I am the business." The first thing I would say is that you need to think about what you've named your business. As a licensed professional, if you have named your business after yourself ("Watson Family Dentistry" for example), you're severely hampering your ability to ever get out of the middle of it. Your name is literally on the building, and everyone will want to be seen by Dr. Watson.

Of course, there are exceptions to this. You could probably name some personal injury law firms that have very famous people as the headliners. It's easy to say, "Well, they're not involved in the daily grind of the business." That may be true, but they're still really involved as the face of the business. If their business was named something more generic that related to the industry as opposed to them individually, that change could help them get out faster.

The reality for dentists, lawyers, CPA's, and others who are licensed as entrepreneurs is that it will take you longer to exit without exiting and to get to the exit lifestyle than other entrepreneurs. The simple fact is that you have to find a licensed person whom you can trust to take over the business when you exit. You still have all of the liability, debt, and insurance requirements. If you have someone acting on your behalf who's not qualified, then you're opening yourself up to a lot of problems.

The bottom line for my licensed professional entrepreneurs out there is this: it will take you longer to get to the exit lifestyle as a licensed professional, but it is not impossible. It's just going to be much more specific. For example, when you embrace delegation, you're going to have to understand who you can delegate to legally, and who you can delegate to ethically to make sure things get done the right way. Then, when you get to the point of investing in people, you need to decide how much it's going to cost you to hire someone with the license to carry on your practice when you are not present. As a doctor, there are many family practices or other medical care practices where there is an attending physician who has some light duties to oversee in the practice, but who is not involved in the day-to-day operations. So you'll need to figure out what you can do to get there sooner rather than later. I encourage you to revisit the story I told about my client, Landon, in Chapter 6 for more perspective on how an attorney can exit without exiting.

The best way to figure this out is to hire a business coach like Landon did. Sit down with a coach and explain to him exactly what you're trying to accomplish, and he will have a better perspective in order to make sure that you put systems in place to allow you the freedom to step away. How long is it going to take you to exit? I can't tell you exactly because it depends on your business and personal circumstances, but here's what I do know. If you adhere to the four core principles as stringent and legalistically as possible for the next six to 12 months, and if you hire a business coach to help walk you through this, your journey will start sooner. You'll also be able to do this with less money out of pocket than if you decide to do so halfway, which will take three to five years of your time.

11. HOW TO MAINTAIN THE EXIT LIFESTYLE

I exited my company in January of 2020. Those of you who are history students will remember that 2020 was the year the world got turned upside down by the COVID pandemic. Certainly, my life would have been a little different and my company's life would've been a lot different. My timeline and the maintenance of my exit lifestyle after I exited without exiting would have been different had COVID not happened. The original plan was squashed when the governments of the world decided to start scaring people into staying home and closing their offices. Our cashflow went to zero in 48 hours in March of 2020. Literally I'll share more on that later.

Nevertheless, I pressed on. I want to tell you a little bit of that story, because I'd like to reflect on how you can maintain the exit lifestyle even in the very worst of conditions, such as in the face of a global pandemic. My original plan was to exit in January of 2020 and to phase myself out of daily operations in the following manner. At first, I was going to have weekly hour-long meetings with my leadership team. That was already our normal operating procedure. Every Monday morning at 9:00 AM, the Executive Leadership Team, or ELT as we called it, would meet for about an hour to cover upcoming projects, administrative policies and tasks. The other items that always had to be handled were things such as employee issues, budgeting, and sales numbers. After that, I would stick around for another hour or two in the office, taking care of other business-related tasks until about noon. Then, I would leave the office and not be back until the following Monday.

I made myself available to the team by phone and through the internal email communication platform, Basecamp, during the week. However, I physically wasn't present except for Mondays during the ELT meeting, at our monthly team meetings, and at family meals. As I explained in Chapter 9, this is when we'd shut the office down on a Friday once a month. We'd have a team meeting in the morning, and then follow that with a catered lunch and play some games for relationship building, culture building, and team building. Then, everybody would go home around one or two o'clock and still be paid for a full day.

Those were the only days each month that I was planning to be present. I was actually ready to become a 10-hour entrepreneur. My next goal was to attend only one of the ELT meetings per month, and then just once a quarter, and then eventually only as needed. That was the plan, and I was able to do this. To this day, I only attend the family meals and team meetings once a month, and I primarily don't have any function other than to be there to talk to employees and take some pictures with people who are getting service awards or celebrating birthdays. Overall, it's worked out very close to my original plan, in spite of the way the pandemic affected everything.

Of course, the timeline worked a little differently, yet I was able to maintain it in spite of what happened with COVID. I was in Destin, Florida, with my wife, daughter, and one of her friends on an RV trip the week of March 15, 2020. It was my daughter's Spring Break of her senior year in high school. On Sunday, everything was fine – restaurants and shops were open and the beaches were jam-packed with tourists all covered in tanning oil. I don't watch the news and haven't done so in over a decade, so I'm not always up to date on world happenings. Sure, before we left on the trip I'd heard about something called "coronavirus" but wasn't yet concerned, nor did I have any idea that it would affect my business. On Monday morning, I had my weekly Zoom call with the leadership team as usual. They expressed concern over how coronavirus would affect importing our products from overseas. I assured them it would be ok, and everyone went on with the day. The following afternoon, I got a call from my VP of Finance. "Boss, we have to lay off four people today or we will be in serious financial trouble soon," she explained. I was not ready for that.

She went on to explain that nearly 100% of our current projects were being halted due to local restrictions on entering buildings. Since having our meeting the previous morning, the operations team fielded dozens of phone calls and emails from customers, telling us we were not allowed to enter their facilities until COVID was under control. Most of our work at that time was in hospitals, so you can imagine how that affected our projects. Without active projects, cash flow died. And it stayed dead for months. I had only been out of daily operations since January, and now due to the shutdowns, lockdowns, government overreach and resulting lack of cash flow, I had to step back in and right the ship. Nevertheless, I was committed to my exit plan and continued to work towards the ultimate goal of my team running daily operations while I explored other projects. As you might imagine, my timeline got interrupted and extended quite a bit, but I still pulled off my exit without exiting, albeit a bit differently than I originally planned.

If I can do this in the middle of a global pandemic, when cash flow is tight and the world has lost its mind, surely you can do it in better times. You simply must make sure that you set up everything so that your business operates consistently and predictably in your absence. There are four main things that you're going to need to pay attention to in order to maintain the business and move into the exit lifestyle. These four things are your team, the financials, the authority or autonomy that you give your staff, and legal issues.

YOUR TEAM

Let's start by talking about your team. As we've discussed extensively in this book, you have to embrace delegation (Chapter 6) and invest in people (Chapter 9). If you've done that correctly, your team should be in place, which means that your leadership should know your plans. They should understand at this point that you are going to step away from day-to-day operations, but you're still present in spirit, so to speak. You must reassure them that you still have 100% authority over the business, you still own it, do not plan to sell it, and you're not walking away or abandoning it. You need to communicate the *why* behind it; that's part of embracing delegation and investing in people correctly.

If you've done this and you've delegated appropriately, your leadership team will be strong in driving the charge on a daily basis – everything from administration, to finances, sales, technology, and whatever the task at hand. They should be ready for this transition. Once the leadership team fully understands your plan, accepts the details, and understands their role, you can begin making sure that the rest of the team is aware of what's going on. If just your handful of leaders know what's happening, but nobody else, they may question where the boss is. *"Where is the owner? Why is he or she not around? What's going on?"* These are not questions your team should be asking. Communicating with everyone at this point is critical, as a lack of clarity leads to confusion and negative outcomes. Negative outcomes in turn lead to failure, and this all can be avoided by communicating clearly to everyone.

I'll give you an example from my own life. I travel quite a bit, and my wife and I take at least a week off per month to go in our RV somewhere. Usually, we take our motorcycle to go riding. On some of those trips, I do some work from the RV because I have a coaching business that I still practice on a regular basis. I also have a mastermind group that I run that's very involved. That being said, there are some trips where I'm absolutely off the grid. I don't talk to anybody, my phone's off, and I'm completely vacated, which is what vacation means.

If your team doesn't understand your lifestyle and what's going on after you walk away physically, it's going to present problems. Since I intended to travel a lot, I had to make sure that my team knew, *"Hey, I'm going to be gone out of town, so if you need me, this is how you get in touch with me."*

After I stepped away from the day-to-day operations, I started several other businesses. Because of that, I made the decision to hire a personal administrative assistant to help manage some of my other companies that were not associated with the main company I exited. She manages all of the administrative tasks for my other companies, most of all my coaching company, TRJD Enterprises. In addition to helping keep those other companies on track, she is the liaison between my main company and everything else I have going on. If there is an emergency or something comes up, everyone knows how to get in touch with her, and she knows how to get in touch with me.

You'll need to set up this same kind of communication network and situate your team so that everybody knows what's going on, what the protocols are, and that the boss (that's you) should only be reached out to in case of an emergency. They should understand that in order to call the boss, there needs to be something very important or urgent going on that has to be communicated right then. You also need to make sure that the communication happens in the proper channels. If it's a true emergency, make a phone call as the first option, and a text message as the second option. An email or a Basecamp message through your internal messaging system is not how you communicate emergencies. You have to make sure your team understands the protocol of how to get in touch with you, because if they don't know, they're going to be confused.

Confusion leads to failure. When people don't know what's going on, things fall through the cracks. So it starts like this: you've got to give great clarity to your team so that they understand. As I said earlier – and it is worth repeating – lack of clarity leads to confusion, confusion leads to negative outcomes, and negative outcomes lead to failure. So if there is a lack of clarity going on inside your business, it's because you didn't clarify what was supposed to be happening. If you want to maintain your exit lifestyle to make sure that your business operates perfectly and predictably in your absence, you first need to make sure that your team has clarity.

How to get in touch with you as the boss is one thing, but something else that's important on the organizational chart is who should be talking to whom. For example, if you have a specific way that you want your employees to ask for paid time off (PTO), then that needs to be made very clear. For example, before I left the CEO role, every employee had to ask their manager for time off. The VPs would also have to ask me for time off for themselves. Since I was no longer going to be present, someone else would need to make these approvals for PTO and VPs. I put in place a protocol that they had to clear time off with each other at their Monday morning ELT meetings, which were their Executive Leadership Team meetings. They had to clear it with each other to make sure they weren't all off at the same time, or they weren't all four working from home when somebody needed to be at the office. The first thing you have to set up and take care of is your team. They have to know what's going on, and they need to have clarity so that they're not confused, which causes negative outcomes and failure.

FINANCIALS

The second thing you need to pay attention to in order to maintain your exit lifestyle would be financials. Understanding financials is a critical part of maintaining the exit lifestyle. If you ignore them when you walk away from day-to-day operations – after you exit without exiting – you set yourself up for a lot of risk and potential legal and financial problems down the road. I had a phenomenal financial controller who was the VP of Finance when

I began my exit. Because of that, I had very little concern or worry about finances. She is a rockstar when it comes to managing finances. She spends the money like it's her own, and that was really important in order for me to feel comfortable walking away from the day-to-day. I didn't have to look at a P&L or the balance sheet every Monday morning to know if we were okay. Instead, I would just check in with Nina on a regular basis to make sure things were going okay.

From a financial perspective, my recommendation is that you should get a month-ending P&L and a balance sheet at the beginning of every month from your finance person. Make sure you understand what the profits and losses both were for the previous month and what the status of your balance sheet is. If you have your eyes on those two things, that is the minimum amount of financial perspective that you need to make sure your business will operate satisfactorily and predictably in your absence. If you see problems, you can call for a meeting with your leadership team to discuss and make sure things get back on track. This shouldn't require more than a couple of hours of your time each month.

Depending upon the type of business that you have, or what type of structure you've set up in terms of your finances, you may also need to look at aging reports, accounts receivable, and more factors. However, those items will be a unique, one-on-one occurrence that you will most likely work with a business coach on. You can set up systems to manage the finances in your absence, but you must remember that from a financial perspective you are still legally the fiduciary for the business. That means it is still legally your responsibility to ensure that your company is financially viable. If payroll doesn't get made, or somebody sues you, or there's a credit issue or a banking issue, it's still going to come back to you. It's best to not abdicate these financial responsibilities. Revisit Chapter 6 for a refresher on how to delegate your finances to someone the right way.

The bottom line is don't ignore it. Stay on top of these things. Your business depends on this, as does your ability to maintain your exit lifestyle.

I'll give this final cautionary note here about financials. One of the things that entrepreneurs do to their detriment – and this goes back to embracing delegation and being the hero – is that a lot of times when a company is struggling financially, the entrepreneur steps in and saves the day. He or she usually does this in one or two ways: either personally loans money to the company or borrows money from somewhere else to infuse into the company when there is a shortfall. Depending upon how much salary he or she is taking as the CEO or the founder, they will sometimes just relinquish some of that salary back to the company for that month in order to help the payroll.

This is a terrible idea, and you should not do that. You started the business to support your life and not just your business's life. Furthermore, your business will never learn how to truly support itself if you step in and save the day financially each time things are tight. It's a common problem and one that can lead to personal and professional hardship.

Reach out to me through my website, *therealjasonduncan.com*, if you want to talk through the details of how this should work. I'd be happy to work with you on how to set up proper procedures for making sure you don't become the financial hero for your company and therefore make it dependent upon you financially.

One of the things I did when I stepped away was to make it very clear that I was moving out. In order to make sure I could exit, I had to also make sure that checks and balances were in place, ensure the payroll didn't have problems, and make sure that there was enough cash flow for people to always be paid. But once I stepped out, it was the ELT's responsibility to make sure that everyone got paid, not mine. Because the ELT was there, it was now part of their job to make sure that everyone got paid.

If the question arose, *"What happens if we can't make payroll? How do we get the money?"* I said, *"Well, then all of us, us meaning everybody – including you and me – will take a percentage pay cut to make sure everybody gets a portion of their pay."* What was never going to happen anymore – which had happened many times in the past – was me forgoing a month or two of pay to make sure that the company had enough cash. In this way, everybody else received full paychecks while I got zero. While you may think this is noble (as I did then), it is actually unethical. I don't mean it is shady or questionable; rather, it is unethical in the sense that it's the opposite of a skillful use of money. This essentially means you are using underhanded tactics to achieve that month's financial goals. By giving away your money to shore up the payroll shortfall, you are lying to yourself. The company isn't supposed to be paid out of your pocket – it is supposed to be paid for the good work and profit created by the company itself. When you swoop in as a hero and save the financial day by taking money out of your pocket, this does nothing to help the company learn how to operate as its own entity. Your baby has to learn to walk on its own. The new rule for me in exiting was, *"If anybody gets paid, everybody gets paid. If somebody doesn't get paid, then nobody gets paid and that includes me as the owner."* While I did reduce my salary and divvied that out to my leaders in exchange for them running day-to-day operations, I still would be guaranteed my income on a monthly basis as long as anybody else was getting a paycheck. To their credit and to this very day, they've never come to me and said they didn't have money to pay payroll. It's funny how that works out…

AUTHORITY AND AUTONOMY

The third concept is authority and autonomy, as these two things go hand in hand. When looking at authority, you have to make sure you've put structures in place to give your employees the proper ability to execute business on a day-to-day basis. For example, if you've been the one who signed all of the checks in the past, you need to designate someone in your company to be the signer. Otherwise, you're going to be spending a lot of time just going to the office and signing checks, which is a silly thing for you to do when you're trying to maintain an exit lifestyle. You need to give someone the authority to do this.

Banks will allow you to put parameters in place where check signing authority has limits. For example, you can set it up where there have to be two signatures. Another method would be to set maximum limits on checks that are signed by anyone other than you. This is a less-secure method, but it is an option. Just set that up so that somebody has the authority to do it. Secondarily, there are contracts that likely need to be signed from time to time, and you don't want to be the signer of these every single time. Somebody has to be appointed to have legal authority to sign on behalf of the company. If you've been the only person to sign contracts until before the exit, you then have to appoint someone else. Who gets authority to sign the contracts needs to be written in the minutes of your business meetings.

For the autonomy side, you have to make sure you've trusted and disciplined them enough to know that you're giving them autonomy to make decisions without you having to be involved. There have been a lot of times over the past years since my exit that decisions have been made about uniforms, or project pricing, or margins, or vendor relationships that I gave my employees the authority and autonomy to make without seeking my approval.

Of course, there are certain things that they have to seek my approval on. For instance, if the company goes into more debt, if there's a line of credit issue, or we need to borrow money, they have to call me. In addition, if there is a personnel issue related to anyone on the leadership team, I must be contacted. Those are not decisions I allow them to make, because ultimately I am the one signing on the dotted line. It all comes back on me if the company can't pay. It's usually a two-minute phone call stating, *"This is why we're doing this."* Then I give them the approval to do it.

LEGAL ISSUES

Finally, we need to discuss legal issues. I've already mentioned this a little bit, but from a legal perspective, if you're an LLC here in the United States, your operating agreement will outline who is responsible as the president and the tax matters member at a minimum. It is still important that you identify who is in charge of legal issues. Ultimately, it's going to be you. From a legal perspective, you can designate people to act on behalf of the company in your absence.

I'm not qualified to give legal advice, so you need to speak with your attorney and say, *"Hey, here's my plan. I am going to exit without exiting. I still want to own the company, but I've appointed people to handle legal stuff on a day-to-day basis. These are the things I want to be involved in. How do we need to write this up so that they have the position to make legal decisions for the company in my absence?"*

As you still own the company and you're maintaining an exit lifestyle, there are going to be times when you can't delegate a legal decision to someone who doesn't have the legal authority to make it. The point here is that you must make sure the legal stuff is handled properly.

If you don't watch these four things and set them up before you exit – team, financials, authority & autonomy, and legal – you will not be able to maintain the exit lifestyle. What will happen is you'll be sipping a drink on a beach somewhere, happily minding your own business, and the phone will ring. Then the emails will start coming in every day, and you'll be interrupted and get sucked back into the vortex of the business that you tried to exit.

You may say, *"Well, Jason, I don't plan on sipping Mai Tais on a beach somewhere! I've got other businesses I want to start. I'm still going to be doing business."* That may be true, but the same principle applies there. You don't want to get interrupted by the old business, while starting that new business. You don't want to end up playing a game of Whack-A-Mole every day when that first company pops its head up every day. Instead, you have to design your systems so your team knows what's going on, the financials are handled a certain way, there's authority and autonomy given to the right people, and legal issues can be taken care of in your absence. If you take care of those four things, you'll be able to maintain the exit lifestyle for a very long time.

I'll finish with this story. My wife worked for the company that I exited for about a year after I exited. She came in to help with some of the administrative tasks after we had to lay off our front office administrative assistant during the cash flow crunch of 2020, and she was happy to do so. The funny thing is she never wanted to do that while I was the CEO, but after I stepped away, she was happy to. As such, all of the employees got to know and love her because she's an amazing woman. She worked in the office for free for a while, and then once things evened back out, she went on payroll. Even though she's no longer officially on payroll for the administrative tasks, she's very much involved. They call her and ask her questions. She's a very smart, kind woman, and they still invite her to the monthly team meetings even though she's technically not on the team anymore. Technically, she'll always be on the team since she owns 1% of the company.

Recently, I couldn't go to a team meeting because I was out of town working with one of my mastermind members on a project. She relayed to me what was covered in the team meeting and what was going on in the company. She then asked me some questions about whether or not I should get involved in some of the things that were going on at the time. I said, *"No, I don't think so. I've worked long and hard to build a business that operates predictably and successfully without my daily presence. Why would I want to insert myself back into that?"*

If I choose to get involved, I can do so. But anytime I put myself back in the middle of the business operations – even just the weekly meeting – I risk being sucked into the vortex of all the day-to-day operation issues. Not only that, but I risk losing focus on the other things I'm doing which are the things that matter to me most right now. I've gone on to start five other companies, and I'm in the process of buying another one. I want to put my energy and time into that as I create generational wealth and create impact for more employees, more family members, and more community organizations through involvement. I can't do that if I'm paying attention to all of the old things in the old business. If I stay out, it continues to run well without me meddling in the day-to-day operations. Yes, I'm eternally grateful for the old business, and I will never take it for granted. It is what I built that allows me to now live the exit lifestyle. I want to maintain this exit lifestyle as much as possible, and I want you to maintain yours in the same way. You can do so by paying attention to the four things I have outlined here in this chapter.

12. LEAVE A LASTING LEGACY

James found himself happier than he had ever been, once he had a company that continued to grow and generate profit without his direct involvement. He was able to be the chaperone on all of the school field trips for his kids. He and his wife bought a short term rental property in the mountains and spent time there every once in a while. It was gorgeous, and everyone who stayed there left genuine 5-star reviews. The best part was that this new investment was throwing off a considerable amount of cash flow each month. He and his wife were closer than ever, because he was able to spend more time at home.

One early Tuesday morning, James was sitting on his back porch, sipping coffee, silently repeating his daily affirmations, and feeling absolutely content with his life. His wife came out to join him in her robe and with her own cup of coffee. They chatted about that week's plans. His wife said, "You know what Michael (their youngest son) said to me last night before he went to bed? He told me that he wants to be an entrepreneur when he grows up." James wasn't terribly surprised at this, because he and his son had spoken about his future from time to time. "When I asked him why he wanted to do that, do you know what he said? He told me it was because entrepreneurs get to spend a lot of time with their families, and employees have to work all the time."

James beamed. His exit lifestyle had made a huge impression on his young son. This was the legacy that James would be most proud of. More than building a multi-million dollar business. More than building a recognizable brand. More than employing dozens of people. The legacy that he wanted to encompass was that he created a business centered around family. What is a legacy? According to the dictionary, a legacy is anything handed down from the past. It could be from your ancestors or predecessor; it could be from an old boss; it could be from anybody. It's usually seen as a gift. The question is, what will your legacy be?

You will leave a legacy as a business owner and as an entrepreneur. If a legacy is something handed down from the past, what is it that you're going to hand down to the people who will be running the business after you're gone? What is the legacy you are leaving for your family? As I've talked about throughout this book, every entrepreneur will exit his or her business at some point. You'll either do this voluntarily through selling it or you'll do it involuntarily through shutting it down, bankruptcy, divorce, legal problems, or even death. So when you leave your business at some point in the future, what legacy will you leave behind? What legacy will remain for your children and your spouse? What legacy will be there for your community? Make no mistake, you will leave a legacy. But what that becomes is completely up to you. Of course, you want your legacy to shine brightly. You want it to be a gift and not only be something that people fondly remember, but also something that they can see had the power to make many lives better. Let's look at the ways you can achieve this type of legacy.

FAMILY LEGACY

One of my favorite movies of all time is *It's a Wonderful Life*. If you haven't seen it, then I highly recommend you watch it. It's an old Christmas movie starring Jimmy Stewart and Donna Reed released in 1946. Even though it is old, it's applicable for any of us at all times in our lives. In the movie, an angel is sent from Heaven to help a desperately frustrated businessman by showing him what life would have been like if he had never existed. The businessman was named George Bailey (played by Jimmy Stewart). George was having some trouble with his business. He was a business owner, and he got into some money trouble and didn't know how to get out of it. He thought that the only way out would be to kill himself so that the life insurance money that would be left behind could cover the money problems. As the story goes, an angel intervenes and tells George that killing himself is not the answer. Even so, George didn't believe it. He was resolute that the only way out of his problem was to kill himself. So the angel gave George a gift by letting him see his entire life story and the impact he'd had on other lives in his town, around his community, and with his family members. The angel also showed George what life would be like in his community and with his family had he never been born.

George Bailey's legacy was turned into an amazing story that he couldn't see while he was still in the middle of his problem. Once he was removed from the problem and got to see what life was really like without him, it changed him forever. At the end of the movie, he went back to his home with his wife and kids. The memories of what it was like when he wasn't around and what life would've been like in the town without him were still fresh in his mind. His family didn't know about his experience with the angel. All they knew was that they were all glad he was back and that he now seemed like a changed person.

The legacy of George Bailey's life comes down to a matter of perspective. It is very difficult in a book like this to give you the full scope so that you can see what a legacy could become for you if you're able to exit without exiting. Don't misunderstand that the exit lifestyle is not just about sitting on a beach, driving a Lamborghini, or having your own helicopter. That's what Instagram wants to tell you that exiting is like, but it's not true. Instead, this is about leaving the proper legacy so that your family, your community, and your employees' lives are improved and better off because of what you built as an entrepreneur. Think about this. What are you going to hand down to your employees and to their families? What are you going to hand down to your children and your spouse? What legacy will you leave?

Think about your family for a minute. What if you make a ton of money but you're never home? What if, like Cheryl, you work 80 hour weeks and eventually sell your business for millions of dollars but miss the most formative years of your kids' lives? You're leaving a legacy in that scenario, but what legacy is that? Let's say you were able to build a business and that business was able to generate $1 or $2 million in personal income for you as the owner every single year. But if the million dollar annual take home salary requires 80 or 100-hour work weeks, what are you really getting? What are you going to spend the money on if you don't have any down time, or if you're never able to enjoy leisure time with family and friends?

I have a good friend who tells a story about the first year or two of his first child's life. He says with regret that he was barely around, and only saw his newborn daughter for about two days during the first year of her life. He was working really hard, building a huge business, and making a lot of money. However, he will tell you, and I will tell you too, that this is not the type of legacy that you want to leave for your family. You don't want your children to say, "Sure, he made a lot of money, but I didn't know him. He made a lot of money, but he was never around. He made a lot of money, but he never went on vacation and when he did, he was on his phone the whole time. He made a lot of money, but he was never involved in any community events. He made a boatload of money, but he missed all of my soccer games."

I'm glad to say that my friend now has a better perspective, and I want you to have a better perspective, too. It would be great if an angel could appear for us all, just like he did for George Bailey. Then, we would be able to see what life would be like without us, or what life would be like if we didn't work 120 hours a week. Obviously that's not going to happen, so instead I want you to put yourself in this scenario. What if you make a ton of money, but you're never home? What good is it doing you? What good is it doing your family?

I ran into a person at a cocktail party not too long ago, and he shared a bit with me about his personal story. He told me that he and his wife were now separated. Then he paused and looked for a moment at me and my wife, who was with me that night. He knew a little bit of my success story and some information about the businesses I had built. He knew that my wife and I had been married for a long time. We had two grown children and life was great. Then he said, "My wife and I are separated because she doesn't understand the entrepreneur's life." He turned to my wife and asked, "How did Jason get you to understand that the entrepreneur's life requires him to be gone a lot?"

She looked at me, and then she looked back at him and said, "He wasn't gone a lot. He was home for everything. There were times when he did work long hours, but he was present, and fully present most of the time."

He looked a little surprised by her answer, and he suddenly seemed a bit dejected. His gaze turned downward, as if he were suddenly thinking with regret. He looked up and asked, "Did I make the wrong sacrifice?"

It would've been easy for me to say, "Yes, you did make the wrong sacrifice. You sacrificed your marriage and your kids for late night entertainment of clients on a regular basis, so much so that your wife couldn't put up with it anymore until she finally had to leave." But I know that's not the legacy this man wanted for his wife and his kids. I know it's not the legacy that he wanted for himself, either. However, every decision we make is a decision that we make. It's not something that's forced upon us. We are not victims of what happens to us as entrepreneurs, or as business owners. Just like this man, we all have to live with the consequences of our decisions. Spending all of those hours entertaining clients and making money isn't worth anything at the end of the day if you don't have your family.

There's no headstone that says, "I wish I had worked more." There's no final conversation with someone on their deathbed saying, "Well, I wish I'd have read those emails. I wish I'd have put together more reports." On the contrary, people on their deathbeds say they wish they'd spent more time with their families, they'd gone on vacations more, they'd learned to dance, or they'd learned to draw or paint. They instead wish they had learned some other hobby or had done something with their kids that they never did.

Recently, at a weekend workshop with my mastermind group called The Exiter Club, I led everyone through an exercise that helped illustrate this perspective about our legacy. This is an exercise you might want to conduct on your own sometime. First, I set the timer for 10 minutes and asked each person to write out the eulogy that would be read if they were to die today. It had to be real and reflect the reality of how they'd lived their lives up until today. After the time was up, I asked for a volunteer to share how the exercise made them feel. One guy named John volunteered and read his eulogy with tears in his eyes, finding it hard to speak at times. By the end, others in the room were crying as well. I admit I was a bit choked up, too. He looked at me and said, "This is not how I want to be remembered."

The second part of the exercise commenced. I set the timer for 10 minutes again and had everyone write a different version of their eulogy. This time, I asked them to write it as they would want to be remembered. Energy flooded the room and pens moved like lightning over the paper as each person began imagining what they wanted their legacy to be. After the 10 minutes was up, there was a brighter mood in the room. John shared his new version, and this time it included all of the wonderful things he desired to accomplish in his life and the impact he wanted to make. This was not only for his business, but for his kids, his wife, and his community. It was a great and joyful experience for everyone.

Your legacy is yours to design. The first eulogy doesn't have to be the one that gets read at your funeral.

It was Jesus who said, "What would profit a man to gain the whole world, yet lose his soul?" In other words, if you've built a great life but haven't paid attention to your spiritual needs and what's truly important in your life, what's the benefit? I'd like to offer a different version of this statement from Jesus for you to consider, as I close out this book. "What does it profit you to make millions of dollars if you are not able to spend time and all that money with people you love and care for?"

I know what you're thinking as you read this: "Yeah, I spend a lot of time working, but I make sure I pay attention to my family. I give plenty of time to my kids." The only way to know this for sure is to get their perspective on the matter. Go ask them in an honest, unguarded, non-defensive way something like, "Do you feel that I spend enough time with you? Do you think that I'm around for you when you need me? Do you feel that I'm always present in your life? Are you happy with our relationship?"

I read an article a few months ago about someone named Graham Cochran. He's an entrepreneur in his 30s who's making about $160,000 a month in passive income. He said that he spends about five hours per week on his business, and he spends the rest of his time with his family. I was so impressed with Graham and his story that I reached out to him and asked if he would come on my podcast to talk about his success. He graciously accepted (episode #089) and we had a wonderful conversation about building a business. But what was even more important to him was how to build a legacy for his family.

It's Graham's type of legacy that we should be aiming for. His kids will grow up with their dad around them all the time. His wife will have her husband there. Essentially, he's developed and built a business and an "exit lifestyle" where he can spend his time paying attention to the things that matter the most. And he's proved that you can do it while also making millions a year.

CREATING GENERATIONAL WEALTH

This isn't to say that money is not important as a part of your legacy. After all, you want your family to be emotionally and mentally satisfied and healthy – which comes from your presence in their lives – but you also want them to be financially stable and secure. This is where sustained incomes come in, which eventually lead to a very important component of your legacy which is generational wealth.

Generational wealth is passed down from generation to generation, allowing families to have access to financial capital and resources to do whatever needs to be done, whenever it needs to be done. Without proper guidance and human interaction, generational wealth will typically be spent by the third generation, after which it will be lost. It's not uncommon to see one generation make the money, the second spend it, and the third lose it. All too often, you find a common trend in this pattern. The first generation who made the money didn't spend time with their kids or spouses. As a result, there was a lot of divorce, remarriage, broken relationships, and splintered families in the period when that first generation of wealth was built. The second generation ends up spending the money, because the generation before made it, so there's a negative connotation associated. The second generation consequently might spend it wantonly and with abandon. By the third generation, there's no connection to where the money came from or how it was built. The money – or what's left of it – is spent without any connection to the original source of the wealth, which came from the first generation. After that, all the wealth is gone forever. This is, to be sure, a legacy. It's just not a good legacy.

I want to encourage the creation of good generational wealth for my clients, which is what I also want to create for my family. My kids grew up watching me as a minister, a teacher, and then an entrepreneur. They saw my life change over time, financially and otherwise. One thing they saw consistently throughout this evolution was that I paid attention to family. While I was not perfect and there were times when I missed things that were important to the family, I made sure they were what mattered the most. Could I have made different choices but also made triple, quadruple the money that I make today? Absolutely. However, that's not a choice that I was willing to make. I wouldn't trade an extra million dollars a year in income for less time with my wife, Kristie.

Kristie is my best friend. I can't imagine walking through this life without her, so why would I spend more time sitting behind a desk, writing emails, doing presentations, and traveling on airplanes just to make more money that she and I can't spend together? In 2022 we celebrated our 27th wedding anniversary. She's the most important person in my life, and we spend a lot of time together. As I said earlier in the book, we take about a week every month to travel, usually in our RV. The reason we're able to do that is because I developed a lifestyle that allows me to.

I am blessed with two amazing kids named Jace and Kiley. I'm very proud of the young man Jace has become. He is a wonderfully empathetic person. I love him very much, and I want to see him achieve everything he desires in life. Recently, he and I have been sharing perspectives on Napoleon Hill's teachings from *Think and Grow Rich*, and the concepts taught by Robert Kiyosaki and Sharon Lechter in *Rich Dad, Poor Dad*. Because of these chats, it's created a tiny spark of an entrepreneurial spirit that I want to help fan into a flame.

Kiley is my Ladybug. Even as a young woman, she will always be my baby. She is in college and hopes to go into ministry, following in the footsteps of her old man. She has developed an amazing group of friends who support and care for her. She doesn't realize how proud that makes me. More than that, at 20 years old, she doesn't yet realize how impactful a good group of friends will be on her for the rest of her life.

I'm hopefully leaving a legacy of generational wealth where my kids will see what's truly important in life. I hope they will see that their Dad worked hard but spent time with them. That he kept his priorities correct, that the center of his life was Jesus, and then his wife and kids, and then the rest of his family, and his community. These are important things for all of us to consider when we think about what the exit lifestyle will bring us.

EMPLOYEE AND COMMUNITY LEGACY

Now, let's shift gears for a moment and talk about the legacy for your business and employees. One of the pinch-me moments of my entrepreneurial life was when I had a moment of awareness that the business I started from scratch was supporting the lives of 12 employees and their families. I was watching employees get married, I was watching their kids graduate high school and college, I was watching their kids get married. I was watching this amazing thing unfolding before me, and to know that this idea and this company that I started was providing income for all of those people was inspiring. The business allowed for the families to go on vacation, for them to stash away money for their newborn child, for their kids to have an education. All of that was nothing short of amazing. I've seen their babies learn to walk, and years later, walk right into my office and tell me about their day at school. The legacy that I want to leave for those people is to make sure that my business survives when I'm not present.

I've started multiple companies, a total of 12 over my lifetime. Each of those has a legacy component built into it for my employees, the contractors and vendors, and everyone else who's ever been associated with the business. I think about one of my employees who now has a son in college. The tuition they're paying for their son to go to college started with a sale that was made in the company I began. In fact, the money they use to pay for their mortgage, their health insurance, their car notes, and all their children's education has its origins in the company I started. It's an amazingly gratifying feeling.

But it doesn't stop there – or at least it shouldn't, if you follow the exit without exiting strategy to create a lasting legacy. One day, that son will get married. He will have his own career based on what he's learning in college and what he saw his dad do in my company. Then, he will have children and they will have children, and so forth.

What I'm saying is that the legacy you're creating as an entrepreneur goes way beyond the money that you bring home personally. It's about the money that your employees are taking home. It is extremely selfish of you to build a business that requires you to be present, because if you aren't present and the business struggles or fails, what happens to those employees? If you build a business that requires you to be there, and then you are not able to be there for some reason, what happens? If the business is 100% relying upon your input, your decision making, and your personality, that sets up danger for your employees. If something happens to you, what happens to that business, to your employees, or to their families?

Remember the study I mentioned in Chapter 5 that was done by Dr. Sascha Becker? It revealed a huge decrease in revenue and profit after the death of a founder, and there was a similar study done here in the US. Both studies found that many businesses closed almost immediately upon the death of their founder, and the ones that stayed open suffered a 60% permanent reduction in revenue. That's a legacy changing problem, and it's not a good one. It changes the legacy of your company and the employees of your company, because everyone was relying on you to be there.

How many people will you affect as an entrepreneur? It depends upon the choices you make. If you make the right choices, you're going to leave an amazing legacy that your employees and their families will remember for generations.

If you exit without exiting and begin living the exit lifestyle, think about the other legacies that can be created outside of your company, your family, and those employees on your team. You could start a nonprofit, you could do mission work, you could spend more time volunteering, you could tutor or mentor underprivileged kids. The potential is endless.

You can also spend time starting other companies that will further multiply that legacy. The exit lifestyle is available to you, and it starts with a choice. You can choose to build your business until you die and hope it will last in your absence, or you can learn the four core principles outlined in this book. This way, you'll be able to leave your business in a place where it can survive and thrive without you. Once it does, your legacy will be enriched, along with all the lives of the people you love and care for.

ABOUT THE AUTHOR

The Real Jason Duncan is on a mission to empower entrepreneurs to discover their true purpose in life by showing them how to run a profitable business in under 10 hours a week. As the founder of one of America's fastest-growing privately held companies and a leading entrepreneurial expert, he draws on his own experience of launching, scaling, and eventually exiting the business he launched as an unemployed schoolteacher in 2010.

Through his mastermind program, The Exiter Club, and his internationally-syndicated podcast, The Root of All Success, Jason teaches the principles of #ExitWithoutExiting, a method for breaking free from the daily grind of business operations and living #TheExitLifestyle. This is an experience that he went through personally in 2020. His professional vision is to see 100,000 entrepreneurs set free from what he calls the ironic prison of entrepreneurship. Jason is also committed to helping 10,000 people escape poverty and mediocrity through the vehicle of entrepreneurship and plans to start a nonprofit organization with the help of his mastermind group to further this mission.

Jason is passionate about coaching entrepreneurs who want to scale, enjoy, and exit their businesses... but that doesn't mean what you think it means! His unique methodology leads entrepreneurs to have complete control over their time and choices daily instead of being in the weeds of business operations every day. The value of this method allows entrepreneurs to maintain the benefit of business ownership–including the financial profits and tax advantages –without the need to be the owner-operator. This is what he calls "Exit Without Exiting".

Before he became an "accidental entrepreneur" in 2010, Jason spent 13 years in pastoral ministry and four years as a schoolteacher. Since then, the businesses he has launched have been featured in several publications, including Inc. magazine as one of the fastest-growing privately held companies in America and one of Entrepreneur magazine's top entrepreneurial companies in America. He owns multiple companies that are involved in various industries, including commercial lighting and electrical services, e-commerce, private lending, consulting services, and real estate.

As host of The Root of All Success podcast, which is syndicated on the C-Suite Radio Network, Jason interviews extremely successful entrepreneurs about their keys to entrepreneurial success. He has spoken at dozens of conferences and appeared on many podcasts. He is a 2x TEDx speaker. Jason is a member of several private and public professional organizations focusing on business growth, personal and professional development, and wealth generation. He is a past recipient of the Rising Star Award from the Tennessee Small Business Development Center, and a nominee of the Nashville Business Journal's Sumner County Impact Awards as well as their 40 Under 40 Awards.

His overall purpose is to use his gifts of teaching and leadership to help others find their true purpose and achieve the results they want out of life.

Besides his professional vision mentioned above, Jason's personal vision is to be known as the kind of man who lived a life that made Jesus and his wife happy. He and Kristie met on a blind date as teenagers and have been best friends ever since. They've been married since 1995 and have two adult children: Jace & Kiley. Jason has lived in the Nashville area most of his life and he and Kristie now reside in Gallatin, just north of downtown Nashville. Jason enjoys riding motorcycles, playing guitar, creating social media content, and exploring the US in his RV with Kristie.

Connect with Jason on Instagram, LinkedIn, and YouTube @therealjasonduncan. Read more about Jason on his website at *therealjasonduncan.com*.

Printed in Dunstable, United Kingdom

81635857R00127